BUSINESS MASTERY

SECOND EDITION

CHERIE SOHNEN-MOE

D1511628

A BUSINESS PLANNING GUIDE
FOR CREATING A FULFILLING, THRIVING BUSINESS
AND KEEPING IT SUCCESSFUL

DESIGNED FOR HEALING ARTS PROFESSIONALS
UTILIZED BY BUSINESS PROFESSIONALS IN ALL FIELDS

BUSINESS MASTERY

A Business Planning Guide for Creating A
Fulfilling, Thriving Business and Keeping It Successful

Published by Sohnen-Moe Associates
3906 W. Ina Road, Suite 200-348
Tucson, Arizona 85741-2295
(602) 743-3936

Publisher's Cataloging in Publication

(Prepared by Quality Books, Inc)

Sohnen-Moe, Cherie.
   Business mastery: a business planning guide for creating a fulfilling, thriving business and keeping it successful / Cherie Sohnen-Moe. – 2nd ed.
   p. cm.
   Includes index.
   Preassigned LCCN: 91-90322.
   ISBN 0-9621265-3-5: $19.95

   1. Business–Management–Handbooks, manuals, etc. 2. Management–Handbooks, etc. I. Title.

HD31.S64 1991   658
                QBI93-20778

Typesetting by DeeAnna Musker-Beckman
Cover illustration and design by Nancy Parker

PREFACE_____

Have you ever wondered why some people seem naturally successful with their work, while others struggle? We've all been told that if you do what you love, then money will easily flow to you. Unfortunately, it's not quite so simple. You need to take action to foster your success.

The purpose of *Business Mastery* is to demystify business, thereby assisting you in having your business be an expression of creativity, joy, empowerment, balance and profitability.

Although this book is written specifically for healing arts practitioners, it's endorsed by business owners in all occupations. Many people embrace the principles and holistic approach to life and business that is the foundation of *Business Mastery*.

Many healing arts practitioners are right-brain oriented (intuitive and creative) and have not learned the skills that are necessary to effectively run a "business". Even those who have been in practice for many years may not have developed these skills. Many talented practitioners are not even coming close to reaching their earning potential.

This second edition is broader in scope than the first book. I have greatly expanded the marketing section: clarified the concept, purpose, and process of marketing; explained how to target your market; furnished examples; provided specific techniques and suggestions for promotion, advertising and public relations; included information on the design of printed promotional materials; and elaborated on the subjects of networking, referrals and client retention.

I have added a chapter on Practice Management that encompasses topics such as: setting your fees, choosing associates, working with employees, developing policies and procedures, and obtaining proper insurance coverage; as well as the activities required in the day-to-day running of your business (e.g., client files, bookkeeping and taxes). Also, you will now find a directory of business resource organizations, a select register of professional associations, a condensed list of Small Business Administration and IRS publications (in Appendix B), and an Index.

Business Mastery is a comprehensive resource tool for use throughout your career. It is designed for those of you who are in business for yourself, work for someone else, are still in school or are just thinking about getting into this field.... Not everyone is meant to be an entrepreneur — but you will always be a healing arts practitioner. And that means that you will ultimately be the one who is responsible for acquiring and retaining regular clients.

This book covers the major aspects of building and maintaining a successful practice. You may find that you only need to concentrate on certain sections of this book, depending on your business experience and the degree of clarity you possess. Some of the topics may not be relevant to you now, but may become so in the future. A chapter on Self Management has also been included to assist you in achieving ongoing success.

Even if you have already been in practice for years, this manual can be extremely beneficial to you and your success. Many people (in all careers) do not have a clear direction for their life, let alone a business plan. Most of those people would be so much more successful and, in the very least, more confident and relaxed if they had a detailed written plan.

It might be appropriate for you to work for someone else for a while, until you build up your financial reserves or business savvy — even though you may want to be self-employed in the future. If that's the case, you will still find this guidebook extremely valuable. It is vital for you to develop a business plan for your ideal business AND your interim phase.

You must decide what you want in life and how your career fits into your wants. In essence, you need to have a life plan, and your career plan is just one spoke in that life plan. Included in this book are sections on life planning and career planning. What you want out of life and the role you want your career to play determine the best way for you to build a prosperous practice and business.

According to a study by Bruce D. Phillips of the U.S. Small Business Administration and Bruce A. Kirchhoff of Babson College, survival rates for service businesses are only average and the percentage of service businesses that grow is below average in comparison to small businesses in general. In doing this study, they have found that two out of five new small businesses actually survive at least six years — instead of the more often cited (but inaccurate) statistics that claim that four out of five businesses fail within five years.

Even though the odds are improving, these statistics still can seem quite depressing. At the very least, they are cause for concern. The two major reasons most of these businesses fail are mismanagement and undercapitalization. Mismanagement is generally a result of poor planning, not realistically evaluating strengths and weaknesses, failing to anticipate obstacles, improper budgeting and not having the necessary business skills. Undercapitalization is not having enough start-up capital or needing to take draw (salary) before the business is firmly established, or both.

Utilizing this workbook will assist you in avoiding some of these pitfalls and support you in creating a successful business.

"To know how other people behave takes intelligence, but to know myself takes wisdom. To manage other people's lives takes strength, but to manage my own life takes true power. If I am content with what I have, I can live simply and enjoy both prosperity and free time. If my goals are clear, I can achieve them without fuss. If I am at peace with myself, I will not spend my life force in conflicts. If I have learned to let go, I do not need to fear dying."

The Tao of Leadership by John Heider

ABOUT THE AUTHOR —

I am a trainer, consultant, author and successful business owner since 1978. My company, Sohnen-Moe Associates, is a full service personal and professional business consulting firm located in Tucson, Arizona. We provide tools and techniques for empowering people in business. I hold a BA degree in psychology from UCLA and have extensive experience in business management, training and creative problem solving — which combine well with my unique ability to motivate others to help themselves get what they want in life.

CHERIE SOHNEN-MOE

I am also a healing arts practitioner and faculty member of the Desert Institute of the Healing Arts. I am an internationally published author, writing articles for several journals and magazines. I am an active member of numerous professional and community organizations. Among my honors I have received the Distinguished Service Award from the American Society for Training and Development, Outstanding Instructor at DIHA, and am listed in several editions of Who's Who.

I am dedicated to supporting people reach the levels of success they desire... personally, financially and professionally.

ACKNOWLEDGMENTS —

So many people have supported me in making this book a reality. Much of the material for this book has been developed and refined over the past seventeen years in my private consulting practice, in courses and seminars I've facilitated, and through my own process of personal and professional development.

I am grateful for the content suggestions, editing assistance, artistic creation, inspiration and general support I received from Margaret Avery, Simi Aziz, Terry Belville, Phyllis Bloom, Jacque Dailey, Kalyn Gibbens, Julie Goodwin, Jamie Lee, Mark Moseley, DeeAnna Musker-Beckman, Lisa Newman, Donna Reed, Carol Simcheck, Judi Spencer, Carol Stocker, Susan Tomlinson, Patricia Warne and my mother Helen Sohnen. Thank you all!

I give special appreciation to Lorie Eufemiese, Mary O'Brien, Nanci Beizer Fink, Janice Hollender, Dominick Angiulo and Barbara Buchanan. Lorie wrote most of the section on Clerical Support Staff and typed the lists of Professional Associations. Mary spent countless hours researching the Professional Associations. The section on Public Speaking contains information from an article that Nanci and I co-wrote. Janice and Dominick supplied me with excellent tax information. The section on Procrastination is based on a column that Barbara and I co-authored for Compendium Magazine.

I acknowledge all of my friends (especially Sandra) who have always encouraged me to pursue my dreams.

Most of all I am so thankful for my wonderful husband Jim. His unconditional love and total support for whatever I choose to do has given me the courage to follow my heart.

Instructions —

Business Mastery has been designed to follow a pattern — the chapters build upon each other, but you may work on whatever sections are important to you. For instance, if you are clear about your goals and direction, you may want to work directly on the business plan. Maybe you have been in practice for a while now: you have a business plan, you know what you want out of life, but you still aren't accomplishing your goals. In that case, you may want to start with the chapter on Self Management.

No matter where you are in your career, if you are willing to take a new look at your life and challenge some of your old thought patterns, then you will find that following this manual from beginning to end is an incredibly valuable process.

It will take a while to complete this manual. Effective planning does take a considerable amount of time and it may seem a bit overwhelming. One way to make this more manageable is to break down your planning into sections and allot a specific amount of time each day to work on each segment. To facilitate this process, space has been provided for you to actually complete the exercises in this book.

One of the major culminations of this manual is the business plan. Even if you decide to skip the previous chapters and go right to the business plan, please read through the entire manual to get a sense of the flow. Some sections include aspects of business that may not pertain to you — such as product sales, group practice, employees or working for someone else. Just review them (someday, you may decide to incorporate those areas) and complete the sections that are appropriate to YOUR business/career.

Appendix A contains copies of some of the exercises and samples of business forms for your future use. Please feel free to make copies of these templates (for your personal use only).

The Self Management Chapter has information and exercises that can be utilized at any time. If you are having any difficulty working through this book, you may want to proceed directly to this chapter.

This is not a manual that you complete and then put on a shelf. *Business Mastery* is a handbook — a resource tool for you to use regularly. It will help you to create the success that you truly deserve!

TABLE OF CONTENTS

Appendix A

Appendix B

Index

Afterword

Other Offerings

CHAPTER ONE

INITIAL CONSIDERATIONS

INITIAL CONSIDERATIONS _____

• INTRODUCTION •

Achieving success in the business world while staying true to the principles of healing and service to others may at times seem like a contradiction in terms. The business world is often portrayed as being heartless, as indeed it can be if you don't know the rules. The exciting thing is that once you do learn the rules, you can choose which ones you want to incorporate in your life and determine how to circumvent the ones you don't like. Many people who choose careers in the healing arts field don't like the business facets at all and thus don't take the time to learn the rules for success or rebel against most (if not all) of the "rules". Unfortunately, that attitude usually doesn't lead to success.

Most people stumble through their lives, not really knowing how or why things happen around them. One of the most important traits that successful people have in common is the dedication to knowledge: Knowledge is power. Self-awareness is the foundation of that knowledge. So, before you even begin to create/update a plan for your career or business it's vital that you assess your current state. It is extremely difficult to know how to get to your destination if you don't know from where you are starting. It is important to include the personal aspects as well as the professional ones. You are a whole being and your career is only one (albeit very significant) part of your life. The exercises found later in this section are designed to assist you in clarifying who you are, where you are right now and visualizing your future.

The diagram on the next page is a completed example of an exercise called the "Wheel of Life". Its purpose supports you in evaluating your life. The chart for you to fill out is on the page following the example. Imagine that the center point (A) is the least desirable state and the outside of the circle (B) is the most desirable state. Look at each category. Take a moment to think about where you are right now. Where is that in relation to where you want to be? Then mark along the line (for each of the ten categories) where you feel you are right now. Next, connect the dots. Do you have a balanced wheel or does it look like a starburst? Keep in mind that it can be very difficult to smoothly roll through life when your wheel (life) isn't balanced.

It is important to consider this wheel from two points of view. First, notice any categories that are proportionately nearer the center than others. Those are the areas to concentrate on improving. What you are aiming to do is bring more balance to your wheel. The second aspect is to enhance all the categories so that they are closer to the outside (most desirable) of the circle.

• WHEEL OF LIFE •

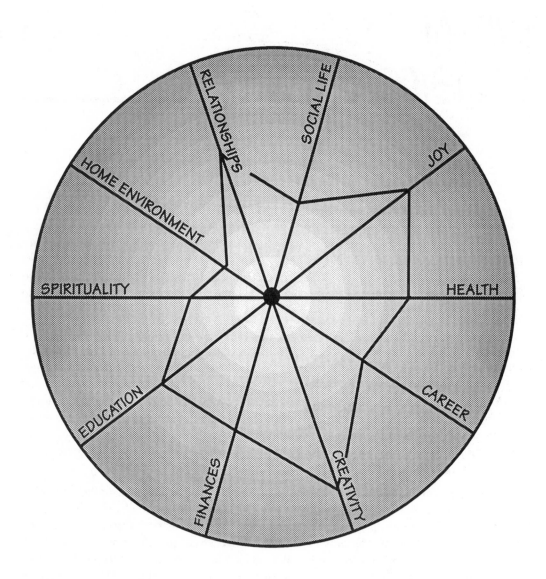

• WHEEL OF LIFE •

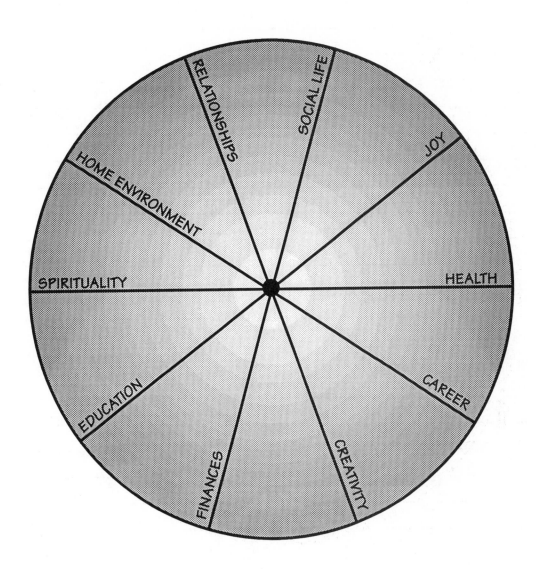

You may want to date this wheel and do this exercise every few months.
It's a great way to chart your progress! A copy of the Wheel of Life is in Appendix A.

• SELF-ASSESSMENT •

Write a biographical sketch spanning your birth to the present. Include personal and family information as well as career details:

_____

_____

_____

_____

_____

_____

_____

_____

_____

_____

_____

_____

List your major accomplishments:

_____

_____

_____

_____

_____

List your talents and abilities:

_____

_____

_____

_____

_____

Describe the current state of your career/business. Include length of time in this field, average yearly income and number of clients:

What is working well?

_____

_____

_____

_____

_____

_____

_____

_____

What isn't working well?

_____

_____

_____

_____

_____

_____

_____

_____

What changes would you like to see occur?

_____

_____

_____

_____

_____

_____

_____

_____

• SELF-EMPLOYMENT •

Many advantages and disadvantages exist in being self-employed. It takes a certain personality type (the entrepreneur) to be truly successful in one's own business. In general, entrepreneurs have a tremendous need to achieve. They are inventive and follow through with their plans. They respect money. They possess considerable expertise in their particular career field and have broad experience in at least several others. Entrepreneurs have very good oral and written communication skills. Most people would consider them as being very personable. The major factor in their success is their attitude — they are positive thinkers!

Some of the advantages of being self-employed are having a potentially flexible schedule, being independent, being your own boss and the potential of receiving tax advantages. Frequently you are able to be more creative and experience increased personal satisfaction and a greater sense of achievement. Being self-employed may also offer you a better opportunity to contribute to others.

Some of the disadvantages of being self-employed are the long hours — usually 10 to 14 hours per day, 6 to 7 days a week. As a business owner, not only will you be working with clients, you will also be actively promoting your practice and taking care of the operational end of the business. In the beginning, you may need to devote 2 to 3 hours in business promotion and development for every hour of client interaction. Sometimes the start-up costs are greater than you've anticipated. Even just printing business cards and mailing notices adds up. You may also experience a deep sense of "aloneness". The income is usually not steady and there are financial risks. Finally, the statistics for success for small businesses aren't exactly inspiring.

Most healing arts practitioners begin their business with very little capital and thus they must build their practice and upgrade their equipment and supplies as the money comes in. It is important to realize that since undercapitalization tends to undermine small businesses, it's necessary to compensate for that lack with other actions. You need to be creative in obtaining services and supplies. If you think that a brochure will attract potential clients, don't wait until you have the money. Talk to graphic designers and printers until you find someone who will do your brochure in trade for your services. You have to be willing to take the initiative. You don't need to know the people ahead of time. When you are attempting to set up a trade, talk to the person face to face, if at all possible. If you are determined to find people to barter with, you will eventually find them. Don't let imagined limitations prevent you from pursuing this kind of arrangement. Your creativity, talent and persistence are the qualities that will help balance out the shortage of start-up resources.

The U.S. Small Business Administration is a wonderful source of information. The people are friendly and do their best to assist you. The following (revised) questions and worksheets are used with permission from their Management Aids MP12.

- Are you willing to take the risks in being self-employed?

- Do you know how much credit you can get from your suppliers?

- Do you know where you are going to get your start-up funding?

- Have you talked to a banker about your plans?

- If you need/want a partner with money or skills that you don't have, do you know someone who is qualified and appropriate?

- Have you talked to a lawyer about your business?

- Does your family support your plan to be in business?

- Have you figured out whether or not you could make more money working for someone else?

CHECKLIST FOR GOING INTO BUSINESS —

Under each question, check the answer that says what you feel or comes closest to it. Be honest with yourself. (From SBA Management Aids MP12.)

ARE YOU A SELF STARTER?

❑ I do things on my own, nobody has to tell me to get going.

❑ If someone gets me started, I keep going all right.

❑ Easy does it. I don't put myself out until I have to.

HOW DO YOU FEEL ABOUT OTHER PEOPLE?

❑ I like people. I can get along with just about anybody.

❑ I have plenty of friends — I don't need anyone else.

❑ Most people irritate me.

CAN YOU LEAD OTHERS?

❑ I can get most people to go along when I start something.

❑ I can give the orders if someone tells me what we should do.

❑ I let someone else get things moving. Then I go along if I feel like it.

CAN YOU TAKE RESPONSIBILITY?

❑ I like to take charge of things and see them through.

❑ I'll take over if I have to, but I'd rather let someone else be responsible.

❑ There's always some eager beaver around wanting to show how smart s/he is.
   I say let him/her.

HOW GOOD AN ORGANIZER ARE YOU?

❑ I like to have a plan before I start. I'm usually the one to get things lined up when the group wants to do something.

❑ I do all right unless things get too confused. Then I quit.

❑ I get all set and then something comes along and presents too many problems. So I just take things as they come.

HOW GOOD A WORKER ARE YOU?

❑ I can keep going as long as I need to. I don't mind working hard for something I want.

❑ I'll work hard for a while, but when I've had enough, that's it.

❑ I can't see that hard work gets you anywhere.

CAN YOU MAKE DECISIONS?

❑ I can make up my mind in a hurry if I have to. It usually turns out okay, too.

❑ I can if I have plenty of time, If I have to make up my mind fast, I think later I should have decided the other way.

❑ I don't like to be the one who has to decide things.

CAN PEOPLE TRUST WHAT YOU SAY?

❑ You bet they can. I don't say things I don't mean.

❑ I try to be on the level most of the time, but sometimes I just say what's easiest.

❑ Why bother if the other person doesn't know the difference?

CAN YOU STICK WITH IT?

❑ If I make up my mind to do something, I don't let anything stop me.

❑ I usually finish what I start — if it goes well.

❑ If it doesn't go right away, I quit. Why beat your brains out?

HOW GOOD IS YOUR HEALTH?

❑ I never run down!

❑ I have enough energy for most things I want to do.

❑ I run out of energy sooner than most of my friends seem to.

NOW COUNT THE CHECKS YOU MADE BESIDE THE ANSWERS TO EACH QUESTION.

How many checks are beside the first answer? _____

How many checks are beside the second answer? _____

How many checks are beside the third answer? _____

If most of your checks are beside the first answers, you probably have what it takes to run a business. If not, you're likely to have more trouble than you can handle by yourself. Better find a partner who is strong on the points in which you're weak. If many checks are beside the third answer, not even a good partner could shore you up.

At this point you still may be uncertain about being self-employed or working for someone else. The next sections on Clearing and Scope are designed to assist you in discerning what you really want in your life and career. Hopefully that will support you in resolving any residual self-employment dilemma.

• CLEARING •

Before you can effectively create your career/business plan, it's necessary to clear the impediments to being able to choose what you want. People are greatly influenced by events that have happened to them throughout their lifetime. Often, they are not even aware of the degree of the impact their past has on their present and future. Unfortunately, a lot of the events and conditions were unpleasant and many decisions and attitudes were developed in response: popularly referred to as "negative conditioning" or "survival skills". Also, conclusions that were made in the past may have been based upon false information or a situation that was only valid at that time. In general, those types of decisions and beliefs are very limiting and do not enhance well-being.

It is not always easy to release negative thought patterns, but the results of doing so are always worth the effort. When you are detached from those past beliefs and attitudes, you can replace them with new supportive thoughts that contribute to having your life be the way YOU want it to be. Frequently, this clearing stage is overlooked (or worse, considered irrelevant) and people attempt to move directly into repatterning. This is one of the reasons why setting goals, writing affirmations, doing visualizations and listening to tapes doesn't always work. Sometimes the conflicts and contradictions need to be unearthed, acknowledged and accepted before they can be replaced. In order for clearing to be truly effective, it must take place on all levels: mental, emotional, physical and spiritual. One of the major principles in clearing is that you must recognize that a block exists and you must be willing to go through whatever it takes to fully release it — even if that means re-experiencing the past buried negativity and pain.

Many techniques are available for clearing. You may decide to use different ones or a combination depending upon the issue. Also, you may respond better to one type of clearing technique than another. Experiment! Some of the techniques for clearing include psychotherapy, bodywork/massage, yoga, rebirthing, some forms of martial arts, energy balancing, flotation, counseling, hypnotherapy, meditation, psychic work and written/verbal clearing exercises. If you do some clearing work and follow-through on your own and still aren't getting the results you want, it may be appropriate to get the support of a therapist.

An example of one of the techniques for releasing the old thought patterns is called "sentence completions". These clearing processes are designed to elicit conscious and unconscious thoughts, attitudes, beliefs and feelings so that they can be recognized and released, thus enabling you to be more free to achieve what you really desire. You can do these exercises alone by writing or verbally with a partner. If you want to do it verbally, have your partner ask you the question(s) and you let your answers come out uncensored. Your partner's role is to keep you moving through the process.

The clearing exercises in this manual are geared towards career, but this process can be utilized for any area in your life.

SENTENCE COMPLETION EXERCISE INSTRUCTIONS —

The following seven pages contain two different questions per page. Answer each question with the first thoughts that come to your mind. Don't try to figure out the "right" answers. It is important to let your thoughts and feelings come out uncensored.

Continue to list your thoughts. Fill the whole page. It is not necessary to write complete sentences.

Occasionally reread the question and list any new or different thoughts. Some of your answers may not make sense — that's okay.

When you think that the list is finished, go over it again. Add any additional thoughts.

Notice any unconscious defense mechanisms that may occur to distract you (e.g., thoughts about the other things you really ought to be doing, how hungry you are, how silly this exercise is, or daydreaming, falling asleep, going blank, etc.). If you are experiencing these defenses, acknowledge to yourself what is happening and then continue with the exercise.

You may find that some of your answers are the same or quite similar for different questions. This is common. It is important to not restrict any of the answers that come up.

EXAMPLE:

The things that are important to me are:

Success

Happiness

Being able to do what I want

Having fun

Feeling good about myself

Movies

Making a difference in the world

Being healthy

Friends

Tacos

Money

Traveling

....

Remember, it might not make sense — but if that's what's there, you must respect it.

THE THINGS THAT ARE IMPORTANT TO ME ARE —

_____

_____

_____

_____

_____

_____

_____

_____

_____

_____

_____

SOME OF MY MAJOR GOALS IN LIFE ARE —

_____

_____

_____

_____

_____

_____

_____

_____

_____

_____

_____

_____

I See Myself As —

_____

_____

_____

_____

_____

_____

_____

_____

_____

_____

_____

Others Perceive Me As —

_____

_____

_____

_____

_____

_____

_____

_____

_____

_____

_____

IF I COULD DO ANYTHING I WANT AND EARN MONEY DOING IT, I WOULD —

_____
_____
_____
_____
_____
_____
_____
_____
_____
_____
_____
_____
_____

THE PEOPLE AND CIRCUMSTANCES THAT INFLUENCE MY SUCCESS ARE —

_____
_____
_____
_____
_____
_____
_____
_____
_____
_____
_____
_____
_____
_____

HAVING A SUCCESSFUL CAREER MEANS —

_____
_____
_____
_____
_____
_____
_____
_____
_____
_____
_____
_____

THE WAYS IN WHICH MY CAREER SUPPORTS ME IN ACHIEVING MY LIFE GOALS ARE —

_____
_____
_____
_____
_____
_____
_____
_____
_____
_____
_____
_____
_____

THE WAYS IN WHICH MY CAREER LIMITS ME IN ACHIEVING MY LIFE GOALS ARE —

_____

_____

_____

_____

_____

_____

_____

_____

_____

_____

_____

IN REGARDS TO MY CAREER, THE THINGS I DON'T WANT TO EVER HAVE TO DO ARE —

_____

_____

_____

_____

_____

_____

_____

_____

_____

_____

_____

_____

IN REGARDS TO MY CAREER, THE THINGS I REALLY ENJOY ARE —

_____

_____

_____

_____

_____

_____

_____

_____

_____

_____

_____

_____

THE THINGS I'M AFRAID WOULD HAPPEN IF I ACHIEVE MY GOALS ARE —

_____

_____

_____

_____

_____

_____

_____

_____

_____

_____

_____

_____

THE WAYS I WOULD HAVE TO CHANGE IN ORDER TO ACHIEVE MY GOALS ARE —

_____

_____

_____

_____

_____

_____

_____

_____

_____

_____

_____

_____

_____

THE THINGS I AM REALLY WILLING TO DO TO ACHIEVE MY GOALS ARE —

_____

_____

_____

_____

_____

_____

_____

_____

_____

_____

_____

_____

• SCOPE •

This section is designed to encourage you to visualize your potential future. Allow yourself the freedom to state your desires, dreams and goals. Remember, this is about your *IDEALS*, not necessarily what you think is realistic.

YOUR IDEAL BUSINESS CAREER DESCRIPTION

1. Where do you want to practice? What city, state or country?

_____

2. Do you want to have multiple locations? ❏ Yes ❏ No ❏ Maybe

If yes, where?

_____
_____
_____
_____
_____

3. Do you want to travel as part of your career? ❏ Yes ❏ No ❏ Maybe

If yes, where?

_____
_____
_____
_____
_____

4. What type of work location do you want?

Do you want to have a private office or work at a medical facility? Do you want an office in your home? Would you rather just do outcalls only? Perhaps you would like to have a combination of the above?

_____
_____
_____
_____
_____
_____

5. How many hours per week do you want to work? _____ Hours

Doing what specifically? In addition to client interaction, include the other business related activities such as marketing, bookkeeping, networking and planning.

_____

_____

_____

_____

_____

6. Do you want any associates? ❑ Yes   ❑ No   ❑ Maybe

How many? _____

What would they do?

_____

_____

_____

_____

_____

_____

7. What type of business atmosphere do you want?

_____

_____

_____

_____

_____

_____

_____

_____

8. How much do you want the net business profit to be annually? $ _____

9. How much money do you want for your salary/draw after taxes? $ _____

10. What benefits do you want your business to have (e.g., health insurance, paid vacations, retirement fund)?

_____

_____

_____

_____

_____

11. What type(s) of people do you want to have as clients?

_____

_____

_____

_____

_____

☐12. Which professions could provide referrals to your business? *

_____

_____

_____

_____

_____

13. For which professions can you be a good source of referrals? *

_____

_____

_____

_____

_____

Please note that although these questions sound the same, they aren't. Of course there will be some duplication, but not always. For example, let's say you are a chiropractor or a massage therapist. A competition weight-lifting instructor might be an excellent source of client referrals. Probably every one of his/her clients could use your services. But, it is highly unlikely that the majority of your clients would benefit from competition weight-lifting training.

14. Describe your *IDEAL* office/location in detail — including external features, the style of decorations, equipment and ambiance.

_____

_____

_____

_____

_____

_____

_____

_____

_____

_____

_____

_____

_____

_____

_____

_____

_____

_____

_____

_____

_____

_____

_____

_____

IF YOU PLAN TO WORK FOR SOMEONE ELSE, PLEASE ANSWER THE FOLLOWING QUESTIONS

15. What is the lowest fee or percentage you will accept? $ _____ or _____ %

16. List at least 5 places or people for whom you'd like to work:

_____

_____

_____

_____

_____

_____

_____

_____

_____

_____

17. Describe the ideal business agreement. What you would like your employer to offer?

_____

_____

_____

_____

_____

_____

_____

What are you willing to provide?

_____

_____

_____

_____

_____

_____

_____

— CHAPTER TWO —

PLANNING

PLANNING _____

• GOAL SETTING •

Now that you have done some earnest clearing work and have considered the scope of your business, it's time for you to set clear purposes, priorities and goals for your life and your business. Goal setting is the means of turning your dreams into reality. This is the main difference between a goal and a wish: when you claim something as a goal, you are stating that you have the confidence and commitment required to make it happen.

Goal setting is tied into the reticular activating system. Our senses (particularly sight) are constantly flooded with inordinate stimuli, yet we are consciously aware of only a fraction of that data. Most of that information is not necessary for our well-being, so it gets screened. In essence, we have programmed directional signalers (or in some cases — blinders) in our brain. Although this may seem like an over-simplification, it's indeed how it functions. For example, recall the last time you decided to get a new car. You finally chose the model and color, and lo and behold! it seemed like everywhere you went, you saw "your car". Now, all of those people didn't just go out and purchase those cars when you did. They were already on the road. You had just never noticed them before because it wasn't significant to you. This is the magnificence of goal setting. By establishing clear goals, you are programming your brain to be aware and notify your conscious mind of the information and opportunities that *YOU DESIRE*.

The inability to realize goals is usually related to unclear goals, lack of commitment, conflict or negative conditioning. Very few people write goals, and those that do, don't always write their goals in a way that easily produce results. Sometimes they write what they think they should want or what their spouse, parent, boss or peers think they should want. Other times they claim to want something, but what they really want is what that "thing" represents. Occasionally conflicts exist in relation to the achievement of their goals. The attainment of one goal may preclude the fulfillment of another, or the consequences may not be viewed favorably by their immediate family and colleagues. Quite often people have a lot of negative conditioning (see Chapter One) that they need to overcome in order to actualize their goals.

Some people write goals that aren't real for them — they "know" that they could never achieve them. Oftentimes they set unrealistic deadlines or have goals that are dependent on other people. Many people have page after page of goals and yet hardly ever accomplish anything. And then some people are so detail oriented that they lose sight of the big picture.

You need a context for your goals, something to connect them. Otherwise they become chores and most people will do almost anything to avoid chores.

PURPOSE provides that context. Purpose is very general — it is a direction, a theme. You can never actually complete a purpose: it is an ongoing process. You may have a purpose for your life and purposes for every major area of your life (refer to the Wheel of Life). In terms of career purpose, take a moment and think about what is really meaningful to you. Are there any common threads — one statement that encompasses your ideals, values and dreams? Another way to look at this is to ask yourself what you would like your clients and colleagues to say about you upon your retirement.

SOME EXAMPLES OF A CAREER PURPOSE ARE:

- My career supports myself and others in being happy and healthy.
- I make a healthy difference.
- My career is a source of joy and prosperity.
- I am innovative and successful in my career.
- My career is a joyous expression of who I am.

You may discover your purposes shifting over time, becoming more refined. Remember that your purposes (and priorities and goals) are not written in stone!

PRIORITIES are areas of general concern. They are less vague and not so all-encompassing as purposes, yet they are not as specific as goals. Priorities are statements of intention that are connected with values.

SOME EXAMPLES OF CAREER PRIORITIES ARE:

- My career provides me with the income I desire.
- I enjoy my work.
- I regularly participate with other colleagues.
- I continually expand my knowledge and skills.
- I am creative in my work.
- My work environment is nurturing and professional.

I suggest you have at least six priorities for every purpose.

GOALS are very specific things, events or experiences that have a definite completion, and you are able to objectively know when you've achieved them. Paul J. Meyers has a great acronym for goals; it's **SMART**: **S**pecific, **M**easurable, **A**ttainable, **R**ealistic, **T**angible.

SOME EXAMPLES OF CAREER GOALS ARE:

- I earn at least $30,000.00 per year.
- I have a wonderful music system in my office.
- I keep my client files current.
- I review my business plan every three months.
- I read at least one business related book each month.
- I am an active member of two business groups.
- I take a 3 week vacation every year.

When setting your goals, I recommend you have at least four goals for every priority.

GOAL SETTING TECHNIQUES —

1. Always state your goals in the positive PRESENT TENSE. If you write in the future, they may always remain in the future — never attained.

2. Personalize your goals: use a pronoun (I, we, they, your name, etc.) in every sentence.

3. Make your goals real: something you know you could accomplish on your own, without help or without someone waving a magic wand over your head.

4. Do not use the terms "try", "will", "not", "never", "should", "would", "could" and "want".

5. Include deadline dates whenever possible.

6. Have fun!

Effective goal setting is the groundwork for success. I advocate that you actually have written goals in addition to any other techniques you employ. The written word is so powerful! By inscribing your intentions, you are saying to yourself and the world that you know you deserve to have these things happen. Sometimes people are afraid to write down their goals because they don't think they can achieve them, and thus they don't want a written reminder of their failures. Failure, per se, doesn't really exist in goal setting. Usually when you don't accomplish a goal it's due to setting an inappropriate deadline, having inaccurate information, experiencing blocks, encountering conflicts, not really wanting the goal or being unwilling (or unable) to do what's required to accomplish the goal. Having written goals can only serve to support and teach you, enhancing your self-knowledge. One of the ways to magnify the power of your goals is to involve as many of your senses as possible (particularly sight, touch and sound) in the process. In addition to writing, you may want to use a variety of methods from visual illustration to audio recordings to physical representations.

COLLAGES are a wonderful way to visually create your goals. To make a collage, you need to first get a large piece of posterboard (22 inch by 28 inch is available in many colors at art supply stores). Then set aside about 2-3 hours, get comfortable, put on some nice music, make yourself a cup of tea, get a stack of magazines, a pair of scissors, some glue and prepare to have a wonderful experience! (By the way, this is a lot of fun to do with friends.) The next thing to do is to decide the purpose of your collage — be it a representation of your whole life, your career, the next six months or even just one major goal. Keeping your purpose in mind, go through the magazines and cut out pictures and words that appeal to you. Let your intuition be your guide. The items you choose may not be what you had anticipated. Don't worry about finding the "perfect" pictures or words. They may be very abstract or elicit a certain emotion. Remember, this is a representation of your dreams and goals. Give yourself a time limit for cutting or else you may find yourself there for days. After you've cut out plenty of pictures and words, glue them onto the posterboard. You also may want to write some goals or affirmations on the board. Then spend some time with your collage — allow yourself to experience the full impact. Finally, hang your collage in a place where you can see it every day.

AUDIOTAPE RECORDINGS of your goals are also very effective. Write out your goals before you tape them, following the suggested goal setting techniques. If possible, use a high quality recording system. The beauty of taping your goals is that you can listen to them at any time. It can be particularly beneficial to listen to your tape while sleeping for the subliminal effects. An interesting alternative is to tape some of your goals in your voice and have someone who is an authority figure to you tape some of the goals. Experiment!

PICTUREBOOKS are also a great way to visually create your goals. The supplies needed are a large three ring binder, a set of dividers, notebook paper, scissors, glue and magazines. Use the dividers to arrange the categories of your goals (e.g., health, finances, education, clients, marketing). Then follow the same directions for the collage, except that you are to glue the pictures and words by category onto notebook paper and then put the sheets in the binder. You may also want to write your goals next to the pictures. The advantages of a picturebook are that you can carry it with you and you can easily add more pages to it. The disadvantage is that you may not look at it as frequently as you would a collage. In any type of goal setting, the more frequently you review your goals, the more likely you are to achieve them.

PICTUREBOARDS are a combination of a collage and a picturebook. Instead of gluing the pictures and words to paper or posterboard, you pin them on a bulletin board. This technique makes it easy to literally shift your goals — put them in different perspective, add more goals and take them down once they've been achieved.

PHYSICAL REPRESENTATIONS are excellent tools for depicting your goal (or goals). The idea is to create a three dimensional object that you can see and touch. This can be very powerful. It makes you really "look" at what you say you want. Generally, it is a time intensive endeavor but it can be well worth it, particularly for the goals that are very meaningful to you and the ones you've been having difficulty in achieving. For example, if one of your goals is to remodel your office, you may want to build a miniature version of your office with all of the proposed changes. Get samples of the paint or wallpaper and put them on the walls. Make (or buy) miniature furniture. Create it as close as possible to your plans. If one of your goals is to exercise regularly, you may want to make a sculpture of yourself exercising. If you are unable to easily recognize yourself, you can always attach a photo of your face to the sculpture. The inclusion of scents adds another potent dimension. For example, if you've been telling yourself for the last few years that you'd really like to take a winter vacation in the mountains, and you still haven't even left the city, it may be that you need to make that goal more tangible. You might want to design a model of the desired location. Start by making a mini-mountain. Then construct a little cabin and inside it put pictures of yourself and whomever else you want for company. It needn't be as elaborate as in "Close Encounters of the Third Kind". Make some pine trees (using real pine needles if possible), and put pine essence on the trees. Now, every time you walk by your mountain, you will be able to see it, touch it, and take in a deep breath and smell the pine trees.... In order to make your physical representation really effective, you need to pay attention to details and make it as realistic as possible. Be inventive and have fun! Do not let a lack of artistic proficiency limit your creativity in visualizing and expressing your goals.

WRITTEN GOALS are a powerful visual (and actually auditory) declaration of your intentions. The two most commonly used methods for goal setting are outline format and mind-mapping. The outline technique is very effective for logical thinkers. When you use the outline format, you write your purpose and your priorities, and then list the specific goals under each priority. The mind-mapping approach is excellent for visually oriented thinkers. In mind-mapping you actually draw the purpose in the center of a page, attach spokes to the circle onto which you list the priorities and then extend lines off of each spoke onto which you write the specific goals. You may find it helpful to use a combination of these two goal setting methods. One of the benefits of having written goals is that it makes it much easier to track progress. The other major advantage of writing your goals is that you can cross them out when they are accomplished — this contributes to a feeling of rewardand acknowledgment.

— Outline Format Example —

Purpose: My career is an expression of who I am.

Priority 1: I continually expand my knowledge and skills.

Priority 1 Goals: Each month I meet with colleagues to share business experiences.

I read at least two business magazines each month.

I take a public speaking course before my second year in business.

Priority 2: My work environment is professional and nurturing.

Priority 2 Goals: I paint my office by July 1st.

I have a wonderful music system in my office by August 15th.

I clean my office every week.

Priority 3: My career provides me with the income I desire.

Priority 3 Goals: I earn at least $30,000.00 this year.

I take a three week vacation this winter.

I increase my client retention rate by at least 20%.

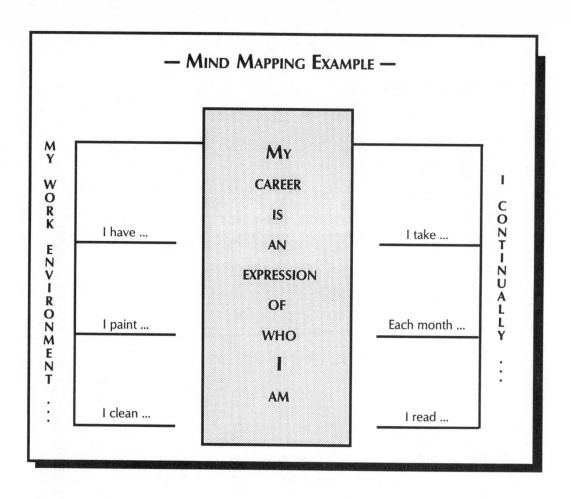

— MIND MAPPING EXAMPLE —

MY WORK ENVIRONMENT . . :

I have ...

I paint ...

I clean ...

MY CAREER IS AN EXPRESSION OF WHO I AM

I take ...

Each month ...

I read ...

I CONTINUALLY . . :

In goal setting, use the format with which you feel the most comfortable and proves the most effective, keeping in mind that it's important to have some type of written goals in addition to any other format, particularly for your career. You may want to use some of the other methods as a means of positive reinforcement and/or visualization. What is crucial is the way you actually state your goals and the individual steps necessary to accomplish them. Be sure to keep your goals **SMART** (**S**pecific, **M**easurable, **A**ttainable, **R**ealistic, **T**angible), follow the suggested goal setting techniques and most importantly of all, be sure they are YOUR goals. Setting goals can be creative and exciting. If you tend to use mainly one method, experiment with other techniques. Use as many of your senses as possible. Goal setting is a necessary component of success, but it doesn't have to be a burden. Remember, the purpose of setting goals is to make your dreams become reality.

Before you even begin to consider developing or enhancing your business, it's imperative to set a strong foundation by clarifying your life's purpose, priorities and goals. Then you can more effectively create your other plans. The following pages are for your use to write your purpose, priorities and goals for your overall life and (then with a focus on your career) for the next five years, three years, one year and six months. Your Wheel of Life can serve as a guide here.

Take a few deep breaths, relax and let your dreams and goals express themselves. Let them guide your mind, heart and hands. For now, don't worry about "how" you write them. Let your creativity flow. You can always go back later and rephrase your goals.

• LIFE PLAN •

MY PURPOSE IN LIFE IS —

_____

_____

_____

_____

_____

_____

MY MAJOR PRIORITIES IN LIFE ARE —

_____

_____

_____

_____

_____

_____

_____

_____

MY MAJOR GOALS IN LIFE ARE —

_____

_____

_____

_____

_____

_____

_____

_____

• FIVE YEAR PLAN •

MY PURPOSE FOR THE NEXT FIVE YEARS IS —

_____

_____

_____

_____

_____

_____

MY MAJOR PRIORITIES FOR THE NEXT FIVE YEARS ARE —

_____

_____

_____

_____

_____

_____

_____

_____

MY MAJOR GOALS FOR THE NEXT FIVE YEARS ARE —

_____

_____

_____

_____

_____

_____

_____

_____

_____

• THREE YEAR PLAN •

MY PURPOSE FOR THE NEXT THREE YEARS IS —

_____
_____
_____
_____
_____
_____
_____

MY MAJOR PRIORITIES FOR THE NEXT THREE YEARS ARE —

_____
_____
_____
_____
_____
_____
_____
_____

MY MAJOR GOALS FOR THE NEXT THREE YEARS ARE —

_____
_____
_____
_____
_____
_____
_____
_____
_____

• ONE YEAR PLAN •

MY PURPOSE FOR THE NEXT YEAR IS —

_____

_____

_____

_____

_____

_____

_____

MY MAJOR PRIORITIES FOR THE NEXT YEAR ARE —

_____

_____

_____

_____

_____

_____

_____

_____

MY MAJOR GOALS FOR THE NEXT YEAR ARE —

_____

_____

_____

_____

_____

_____

_____

_____

_____

• SIX MONTH PLAN •

My Purpose For The Next Six Months Is —

_____

_____

_____

_____

_____

_____

My Major Priorities For The Next Six Months Are —

_____

_____

_____

_____

_____

_____

_____

My Major Goals For The Next Six Months Are —

_____

_____

_____

_____

_____

_____

_____

_____

_____

• STRATEGIC PLANNING •

CONGRATULATIONS!!! You now have written your intentions for your life and created your purposes, priorities and goals for your career. Having built this foundation puts you miles ahead of the general public and well on your path to success. Just writing some of your goals may be all the planning you need to do — given that you actually do them.

But some of your goals may be very complex and each goal might have numerous substeps necessary to accomplish the goal. This process of "divide and conquer" (i.e., breaking down a difficult problem into manageable chunks), is where strategic planning comes in.

Strategic planning is an extension of goal setting — the actual writing procedures are the same. The difference lies in that it is a whole plan, not just a simple goal. An example of a goal that could need a strategic plan is, "I pass my certification exam by May 4, 19___." Many steps have to be made in order to accomplish this goal. Some of those steps include studying, applying for the exam, taking any necessary reviews, being tutored in weak areas and practicing. This example has only a relatively few steps required to accomplish the goal, but it doesn't matter if a plan has three steps or thirty — the process is still the same.

You may even find that when creating a strategic plan, one or more of the steps requires a strategic plan of its own. This usually only occurs with major, complicated goals. Most goals are not like that, they tend to be rather straightforward.

CREATING STRATEGIC PLANS PROVIDES MANY BENEFITS —

1. You are less likely to forget a major step if you have it written down.

2. You are more able to brainstorm creative ideas.

3. Your goals become clarified and more "real".

4. You get a better overall picture.

5. You become more able to see how some steps may require immediate action over others, even though they might not hold the same personal value significance.

6. You know what is necessary to accomplish the goal.

7. You develop a more accurate time table.

8. You have a written description of your intentions that can serve as a wonderful self-motivational tool.

On the following pages is a sample of a completed strategic plan using the goal of "I earn at least $30,00.00 (after taxes) this year." Blank copies of the strategic planning sheets can be found in Appendix A.

STRATEGIC PLANNING SHEET —

TODAY'S DATE: Jan 15   **TARGET DATE:** Dec 31   **DATE ACHIEVED:** _____

PURPOSE: My career supports myself and others in being happy and healthy.

PRIORITY: My career provides me with the income I desire.

SITUATION DESCRIPTION: I have been in practice for less than two years. I am billing almost $50,000.00 per year, yet after expenses, my pre-tax income is less than $25,000.00.

OBJECTIVE: Change this condition.

GOAL: I earn at least $30,000.00 (after taxes) this year.

BENEFITS OF ACHIEVING THIS GOAL: I can pay off my debts. I am able to have the lifestyle I want. I am able to afford to build up my practice. I can take a vacation this year! I can buy some new clothes. I am able to start a retirement account. I am able to afford to take educational courses.

POSSIBLE COURSES OF ACTION:
1. Increase the number of clients.
2. Raise my rates.
3. Diversify.
4. Decrease expenses.

BEST COURSE: Currently, the most appropriate action to take is to expand my client load, which includes increasing client retention.

PROPOSAL/OUTLINE:
1. Review client files. Implement a customer service plan to increase client retention.
2. Design an effective marketing plan to get new clients.

ADVANTAGES: Clients are the cornerstone to any business. I will concentrate first on enhancing my relations with my current clients, since it's more cost effective in terms of money and time to keep the clients I already have, than to get new clients. Also, satisfied clients will recommend me to their friends. In the meantime, I will develop effective marketing strategies for attracting new clients.

POTENTIAL CONFLICTS/DISADVANTAGES:	**SOLUTIONS:**
1. Not having enough clients.	1. Increase client retention. Develop a great marketing plan.
2. Having to spend more money than anticipated.	2. Do an accurate budget and stick to it.
3. Possible emergencies.	3. Ask for support.
4. I may have to work too many hours and not have enough personal time.	4. Set goals for personal time. Do daily time tracking. Get a coach.

ACTION REQUIRED TO BEGIN: I need to gather my files and review them. I must set aside a block of time to do the actual planning.

RESOURCES NEEDED: Time, paper, pencils, a quiet place and ultimately an advisor to review my plans.

SPECIFIC STEPS TO ACHIEVE THIS GOAL   TARGET DATE

1. I reserve a date and location to do my initial planning — Jan 17

2. I gather all my records and files. — Jan 19

3. I review my files and revamp my business plan. — Jan 20

4. I get clear on my high priority activities. — Jan 26

5. I set up a tracking system. — Jan 31

6. I create a realistic budget (and stick to it). — Jan 31

7. I contact the experts in my field to get current trends. — Feb 10

8. I contact the Chamber of Commerce for statistics. — Feb 10

9. I develop and implement a customer service plan. — Feb 13

10. I complete the research on local competition. — Feb 17

11. I go to the bookstore and buy books. — Feb 19

12. I talk to at least three established practitioners (in my field) to get their perspective. — Feb 20

13. Each month I do a presentation or demonstration for a professional/business group. — by Mar

14. I join (or start) a business support group. — Mar 31

15. I read at least two business books. — Apr 10

16. I attend a business development seminar. — Apr 18

17. I create an effective marketing plan. — May 15

18. I meet with a business consultant to review my plans. — May 20

19. I implement my marketing plan. — May 24

20. I write daily goal and affirmations. — Always

• FOLLOW-THROUGH •

Creating your life to be what you want is an ongoing process. In terms of goal setting, the actual statement (written, verbal and pictorial) of the goals is only one step. In order to increase the potential of achieving the goals, it's important to incorporate clearing, strategic planning, prioritization, tracking, affirmations, visualization and self-acknowledgment.

So far we have covered clearing, goal setting and strategic planning. Tracking and prioritization are techniques to assist you in staying on target and are discussed in the chapter on Self Management. The rest of this section is focused on affirmations and visualization.

VISUALIZATION —

The concept of visualization has been one that has inspired many people and accelerated their ability to change their lives, yet for others has been a source of frustration. A popular saying goes "If you can't see it then you'll never be able to have it." That statement is true, but only in its purest sense. Not everyone "sees" the same way. When some people envision a goal they don't actually see it, but they get a physical sensation or they hear the sounds associated with the goal. For example, let's say that you have a goal to go on a hike this weekend. You may actually see yourself waking up in the morning, getting dressed and walking through the hills — fully seeing the surroundings. Another possibility is you might feel how it is to be hiking — the stretching of your muscles, the smell of the flowers and the emotional interaction you have with the environment. Finally, your "visualization" might be verbal. You may actually talk yourself through the day or even imagine the sounds of the animals, the wind and the conversation of the others on the hike. Your visualization may also include a combination of sight, sound, smell and sensation.

Ultimately, the more senses you can incorporate into your visualizations, the more powerful they become. You can visualize in your head — with or without closing your eyes, you can use the methods described under goal setting techniques or you can create your own process. Another option using a visual representation is to carry a picture of the goal. For example, if you want a new car, have someone take a picture of you sitting in the exact model you desire or cut out a picture of the car from a brochure (and possibly glue on a picture of your face in the driver's seat). It is not necessary to "visualize" in any specific way. Do what works best for you. The possibilities for creativity are abundant!

AFFIRMATIONS —

An affirmation is a positive declaration that something is already so. It can be general or very specific. It is a constructive thought that you deliberately choose to place in your consciousness to produce a desired result. The purpose of writing/saying affirmations is to support you in actualizing your dreams and goals by replacing negative self-talk with positive self-talk. When you create affirmations, you are in essence planting a seed for new beginnings. Avoid becoming attached to the specific details of "how" the affirmation will manifest. As with goal setting, always state your affirmations in the positive present tense and personalize them. Choose affirmations that feel good to you. What works for one person may not work for you.

Affirmations can be used in many ways to produce powerful results. Experiment with some of the following suggestions:

- Read your affirmations at least three times per day.

- Write each affirmation 10 to 20 times in succession.

- Write your affirmations while speaking them aloud to yourself.

- Write your affirmations in the first, second and third person.
  For example: "I, Sue am healthy." "You, Sue are healthy." "She, Sue is healthy."

- Write your affirmations and tape them up (or use Post-it notes) around your home, car and office. Put them on the telephone, the refrigerator, your desk, mirrors, doors, over your bed and on the dashboard.

- Make bookmarks with your affirmations on them.

- Record your affirmations on tape and listen to them as you drive, exercise and before you go to sleep.

- Meditate on your affirmations.

- Stand in front of a mirror and look at yourself while saying your affirmations.

- Take turns saying and accepting affirmations with a friend.

- Make flash cards with your affirmations and carry them with you.

- Design or buy clothes with affirmations on them.

- Sing or chant your affirmations.

Doubts, resistance and physical discomfort are a natural side-effect of the affirming process. If you notice these feelings while you are creating an affirmation, do not fight them. Accept them, acknowledge them and allow their expression. Sometimes these feelings are signals of deep conflicts that may require more (or other types) of clearing. You may be able to discharge the negative energy by doing the following clearing exercise. Write down the affirmation on a piece of paper and then write the response that comes to mind. Then rewrite the affirmation and the next thought that comes to mind.

For example:

I, Bill, love my life! .... **Sure bet.**

I, Bill, love my life! .... **But not my job.**

I, Bill, love my life! .... **Not right now I don't.**

I, Bill, love my life! .... **Maybe someday — if I win the lottery.**

I, Bill, love my life! .... **I just wish it wasn't so painful.**

I, Bill, love my life! .... **Hmmmm.**

I, Bill, love my life! .... **I see the possibilities.**

Continue writing the affirmation and your reactions until you no longer elicit negative responses. Do this for several days or until you feel you've discharged the negativity. Now you can return to working with the original affirmation. This exercise can be time consuming, but you are worth it! Affirmations are most effective when the path is clear of resistance.

SAMPLE AFFIRMATIONS —

I am the master of my life.

I fully love and accept myself as I am.

I am a dynamic public speaker.

I live up to my own highest ideals.

I see the opportunities in life.

I always communicate clearly and effectively.

I am a radiant powerful being.

I am happy!

I manifest my power with integrity and love.

I am vibrantly healthy.

My life is a joyous adventure.

I am creative in all that I do.

My career supports me in being who I am.

My relationships are nurturing and fun.

I am aligned with the divine plan of my life.

I appreciate the good in my life.

I am in an exciting romantic relationship.

I allow people to support me and they do.

I have the time, energy, wisdom and money to accomplish my goals.

My career is fulfilling and prosperous.

The more abundance I have, the more I have to share.

I am well organized.

I am true to myself.

My creativity is flowing and focused.

My life is a continual expansion of joy and aliveness.

Everything I need is already within me.

Every dollar I circulate returns to me multiplied.

I trust my intuition.

My life is filled with laughter and love.

CHAPTER THREE

BUILDING A
STRONG FOUNDATION

BUILDING A
STRONG FOUNDATION___

• INTRODUCTION •

Being current with the specific skills in your field is vital in developing and maintaining a thriving practice. Stay up-to-date with the trends, read all of the new literature, take seminars and learn new techniques.

One of the most effective ways to keep knowledgeable on different techniques is to make sure that you experience sessions by others in your particular profession on a regular basis — preferably at least once per week (although this can be difficult if you are a dentist, for instance). Even if you have a favorite person to go to, try out others. Remember you are getting these sessions not only for the direct benefits but also as a means of experiencing other techniques. You may discover a technique that is absolutely wonderful and then you can take the necessary steps to learn it. Receiving these treatments on a regular basis assists you in being more attuned to your clients' needs.

It is also helpful to be assessed periodically. This can be done by your clients and by colleagues. Some healing arts practitioners have every client fill out a form for every session and others go through this process only once or twice per year. Feedback is essential for your professional progress. This concept can seem a bit scary — the idea of being evaluated does have some ego risk involved, but how are you going to know which areas to enhance if no one tells you. Remember, knowledge is power. Since most work in this field is very individualized, it's recommended that you obtain as many evaluations as possible in order to get broader, more objective feedback. These evaluations are for your benefit. They are also a good way to get your clients involved in their treatment (see client retention and motivation).

Getting assessed by your colleagues is very important. They can give you the kind of technical feedback that a client probably would not know. Again, it's not necessary to be evaluated every time you work with your peers, but do it regularly. You can also make it fun. Your purpose is not to "find fault" but to support each other in being the best you can be.

Healing arts practitioners are not often "business" inclined. These are skills that are developed through practice and discipline. It is not enough to be an excellent practitioner. You also need to be a competent business person. Some of the business skills involved in a healing arts practice are knowing how to: communicate well, develop a professional image, keep client files, write a business plan (Chapter Six), create strategic plans (Chapter Two), prepare an introduction or résumé, manage yourself and your business (Chapter Four), handle an employment interview, keep books, ascertain the ordinances in your area, retain clients and promote your business (Chapter Five).

These business skills are fundamental to your success — whether you work for someone else or are self-employed. It is beyond the scope of this book to thoroughly educate you in all of these areas. Some skills are extremely difficult to illustrate in a book. For example, it's hard to demonstrate the delivery components in public speaking. Other topics, such as insurance reimbursement (Chapter Four), may require several books to cover procedures and codes. And hundreds of books can be found on communication skills. The intent here is to convey to you the fundamentals for business success and to familiarize you with the other principles and skills so that you can appropriately decide which areas you want or need to pursue.

• GOODWILL AND PROFESSIONALISM •

Goodwill is an integral component for success in any service industry, and especially so in the healing arts field. Goodwill is defined as benevolence, friendly disposition, cheerful consent, willingness and readiness. In regards to business it is the commercial advantage of any profession due to its established popularity, reputation, patronage, advertising, location, etc., over and beyond its tangible assets. In other words, goodwill is an abstract impression, the "positive feelings" you inspire in others. It is based upon the supposition that you are doing the best you can and will be fair and ethical in your dealings and behavior.

Take a moment to think about the businesses and people that you respect. Why do you hold them in this regard? What have they done to encourage these feelings of goodwill? How have they demonstrated their concern? Your responses are the key to understanding the concept of goodwill.

It is essential to cultivate alliances. Many branches of the healing arts have substantial distances to cover before they get the recognition they deserve from the general public and the health industry. A major part of this guarded acceptance stems from having no set protocol. The general public still doesn't know what to expect. The variety of styles, modalities, philosophies and fee structures are as diverse as those who practice them. In order to gain further headway for recognition, it's imperative to enhance the public image of this field — in other words, promote more goodwill.

The healing arts field tends to rely on attraction rather than traditional methods of promotion, (e.g., word-of-mouth, reputation and client referrals). The downside to this is that word-of-mouth often revolves around "who" you know more than "what" you know. And even then, it isn't enough to just know the "right" people. In order to obtain their support, you need to nurture those associations. You must have good people skills. For example, you could be the most brilliant practitioner or therapist in your area, yet if you don't promote goodwill with your clients, centers of influence, colleagues and the community, you still may not do well financially. One of the most important habits to develop is the prompt and gracious acknowledgments of all of the people that support you. A little recognition goes a long way!

It takes time, thought, creativity and some money to foster goodwill. Being good at what you do is only one aspect of it. Make certain that your actions reflect that you are proud of your profession and are sincerely concerned about people's well-being.

You can't buy goodwill, particularly if it is an attempt to repair a bad reputation (although many corporations have spent millions of dollars attempting to do just that). But you can bolster the general public's opinion of you and your profession by donating your services and knowledge to charitable organizations and events — especially if you get media coverage.

Establishing goodwill begins with your commitment to exhibit professionalism. Professionalism stems from your attitudes and is manifested through the image you portray, your technical skill level, your communication abilities and your business practices.

No matter how many hours you work, this is your profession. There is a major distinction between part time and spare time. You may have other facets to your career besides being a healing arts practitioner, but it's important to be clear about the roles each facet plays and be committed to excellence in each area. Quantity does not determine quality.

You are a healing arts professional, but foremost you are a business person — even if you only work 3 hours a week. The more you treat your practice as a business, the more professional you will appear and the more successful you will become. Sometimes this can be difficult, particularly if you do not have a lot of technical business experience.

Many people become trained in the healing arts professions because they enjoy the intuitive creative nature of this career field. It can be very distressing when they discover the degree to which they have to be involved in the business world in order to have a successful practice. But this too can be creative and fun, once you know the rules. Business Mastery was created to assist you in learning the fundamentals of creating a successful business.

Your attitudes towards yourself and your business get communicated directly and indirectly to your clients, colleagues and potential clients. You need to respect yourself and your abilities.

The basis for true professionalism lies in integrity. Webster defines integrity as the quality or state of being complete; unbroken condition; wholeness; honesty; and sincerity. Integrity is often considered as a thing to have — people have integrity if they are ethical, can keep confidences and keep their word. But there is more to it than that. Integrity can be divided into three major levels: the first level is keeping your agreements; the second level is being true to your principles; and the third level is being true to yourself. Integrity is a state of being and if that is where you are really coming from, you are professional.

PROFESSIONAL CHARACTERISTICS —

THINK ABOUT SOMEONE YOU REGARD AS BEING VERY PROFESSIONAL

- What is this person's occupation?
- What is his/her philosophy of life?
- How does s/he feel about his/her career?
- What does s/he look like?
- Where is his/her place of business?
- What does it look like from the outside?
- Can you easily see it from the street?
- Is parking easily accessible?
- What does the office look like?
- How does this person greet you?
- What does s/he say and do?
- How do you feel?

TAKE A FEW MOMENTS TO THINK ABOUT WHAT PROFESSIONALISM REALLY MEANS TO YOU.

Describe yourself in terms of professionalism:

_____

_____

_____

_____

_____

_____

_____

_____

Describe how you imagine others see you in terms of professionalism:

_____

_____

_____

_____

_____

_____

_____

_____

List any of the changes you would like to make:

_____

_____

_____

_____

_____

_____

_____

_____

Professionalism isn't measured by how many clients you see or how much money you earn but rather by who you are, your attitudes and how you treat others.

• IMAGE •

Once you have established a strong foundation of professionalism by developing a healthy attitude towards yourself and your career, you can take steps to increase your goodwill by improving your public image. Your public image is determined by the way you present yourself, your office, your business practices and the manner in which you treat your clients. The following lists are etiquette guidelines to bolster your image and reputation.

YOU ARE YOUR BUSINESS. YOU NEED TO EXUDE CONFIDENCE, COMPETENCE AND COMPASSION:

- Dress stylishly yet neatly, and keep jewelry to a minimum — your attire isn't meant to be a distraction or a loud statement.

- Keep good personal hygiene and don't wear heavy perfume or cologne — you don't want to bring tears to your clients' eyes.

- Keep your technical skills excellent and current — do not pretend to be an expert in what you're not.

- Be punctual and prepared — make your clients feel important and respected.

- Know how to introduce yourself and others — it can be very embarrassing if you stumble over your own tongue.

- Get involved in your community — become active in civic, social and political groups.

MAKE CERTAIN THAT YOUR OFFICE SPACE GENERATES A COMFORTABLE YET PROFESSIONAL AMBIANCE:

- Be aware of the noise level and make any necessary adjustments — turn off the phone bell, soundproof thin walls, etc.

- Keep the interior clean — particularly the bathroom.

- Make sure that the building and address is visible from the street — this may mean investing in signage.

- Maintain the area outside your office — this may include landscaping.

- Keep the temperature comfortable for the client — if you don't have easy access to the temperature control, put a portable heater and fan in the room.

- Create a sense of privacy — you may have to be very inventive.

- Make certain that all equipment and furniture is comfortable and sturdy —you do not want a table to collapse under a client!

- Provide closet space or a shelf (at the very least, a hook) for your clients' belongings — most people don't like to throw their possessions in a corner.

- Keep supplies stocked and handy — you don't want your clients having to search for a tissue while they're sneezing.

- Post your business license, policies and awards, etc., in a conspicuous place — these items represent the time and effort you've invested in your career.

- Have your business cards and literature available — make it easy for your clients to take what they need to help promote your business.

THE MANNER IN WHICH YOU RUN THE "BUSINESS" PART OF YOUR PRACTICE DIRECTLY AFFECTS YOUR LONG TERM SUCCESS:

- Answer your phone professionally — you don't have to be overly formal, but remember you are a business. If you don't have a receptionist, I advocate hiring a reliable appointment service. They can significantly increase your bookings.

- Return calls within 24 hours — you never know the influence and connections that a potential client may have; promptness is always appreciated.

- Answer important mail within 4 days and nonessential mail within 2 weeks — don't wait until you have the time to write a brilliant letter. (I always keep a supply of postcards handy. This way I can quickly acknowledge correspondence without worrying about having to fill up the page or making sure my typewriter is working.)

- Send newspaper clippings, articles and items of interest to clients and colleagues — this lets people know that you are thinking about them and are genuinely concerned.

- Acknowledge in writing any item or gift sent to you — thanking people over the phone is okay, but people usually keep cards for several days. Every time they look at your card, it reinforces their feelings of goodwill.

- Send thank-you notes for referrals — it's vital to show your appreciation, particularly since many people aren't totally comfortable telling others about the health care methods they utilize.

- Set clear boundaries — don't let your personal life interfere or intrude with business.

- Return borrowed property promptly and in good condition — never borrow anything that you are unable to replace (in case you damage or lose it).

- Never repeat a rumor that could hurt someone's reputation — it's wise to stay neutral. Gossip never reflects well on any of the parties.

- Keep accurate client files — review them before you see each client. Don't rely on your memory for all the details of your last session.

THE WAY IN WHICH YOU TREAT YOUR CLIENTS DETERMINES WHETHER OR NOT THEY BECOME REGULARS:

- Be empathetic and understanding — keep in mind that not everyone shares your particular beliefs about health and well-being.

- Greet your clients appropriately — some people may not be up to a bear hug.

- Keep what happens during a session confidential — this can be tricky when your clients know each other and ask about the other's appointment. Be noncommittal and recommend they speak to the person directly. Even a casual remark can damage your trust factor.

- Remember that you are here to serve your clients — it isn't their job to counsel you during their sessions.

- Be observant of your clients' likes and dislikes — make the effort to do those "extra little things".

Your level of integrity, professionalism and grace determine how you are perceived. Taking the time to project a professional image is always worth the investment. It is not necessary to have a huge promotional budget either — just creativity. Most of the above guidelines don't involve any financial outlay. The desired result is that your image is professional, and it's vital that you don't lose yourself in this process. Who you are is what makes you good at what you do. It distinguishes you from the others. Keep your style and personality intact.

• COMMUNICATION SKILLS •

Communication skills are an integral component of your profession. When you are with a client, you need to be able to listen with all of your senses. When you are promoting your business, you must be able to clearly explain what you do. Some of the benefits in honing your communication skills include: improved results for your clients, time saved in resolving any misunderstandings, improved cooperation and teamwork, increased productivity, reduced stress and increased satisfaction.

THE FUNDAMENTALS FOR GOOD COMMUNICATION

1. Take into consideration the person's natural tendencies and capacities. For example, if someone prefers to see things in writing, don't expect him/her to be very responsive to verbal communications. Also, if you are talking to someone who doesn't speak English well, avoid using polysyllabic words and rapid speech.

2. Be considerate of the other person's mental, physical and emotional state; particularly if s/he is under a lot of stress.

3. Communicate on an equal level. Don't act superior or inferior.

4. Be honest.

5. Know his/her opinion of you. If someone fully respects your expertise, it isn't necessary to take the time to build up your credibility. But, if s/he doesn't know you, you need to take the time to build rapport and trust.

6. Have good timing. As "they" say, timing is everything!

7. Separate your emotions from the facts. It is difficult to have clear communication when you are coming from a reactionary position.

8. Ask questions.

9. Listen. Listen. Listen...

You can improve your communication skills in many ways. The most important thing to remember is that people act and react in order to fulfill needs. When you better understand their needs, you will be able to create a better strategy for improving communications.

Seek to understand — not to be understood

• EMPLOYMENT INTERVIEWING SKILLS •

It is wise to learn interviewing skills — even if you are or plan to be self-employed. Much of the basics in being adept at interviewing center around having excellent communication skills. You must be confident, and most important of all, you must be prepared. Many good books are written and several companies facilitate seminars on this topic. The list below contains some of the components of successful interviewing skills.

- Be well poised, centered and relaxed.
- Maintain good eye contact.
- Listen to what is really being said.
- Dress appropriately.
- Use positive wording.
- Take control of the interview.
- Avoid telephone interviews.
- Ask specific questions and don't give vague answers.
- Look for closing signals.
- Avoid discussing salary and benefits in the first interview.
- Be prepared. Have all necessary documentation available.
- Bring an appointment book and a classy pen.
- Be on time.

After you have honed your interviewing skills, you must learn how to get an interview.

- Create a list of potential employers. Get their addresses, phone numbers and the names and titles of the people who have hiring authority.
- Network. Network. Network. Talk to people, let them know you're available. Ask for leads. Remember, quite often it's who you know that gets you the job. (Chapter Five has more specifics on networking.)
- Set up initial contact on the phone. You must be well organized, know your purpose and goals for this call. The primary goal, of course, being to get an interview.
- If you don't get an interview from this initial contact, send a résumé with a cover letter or just send a letter.
- If you have not gotten a response within five days of them having received your letter, call them.
- In some cases, endurance pays off. If you keep yourself so visible that an employer is fully aware that you really want to work for his/her company, you may get the job out of sheer persistence.

Before your actual interview, prepare yourself. Research the company. Know how long it's been in business, the number of employees, the services it offers.... Be ready with answers that the employer is likely to ask. Roleplay the potential interview with a friend. Get feedback. Make any changes necessary so that you can have an excellent interview.

• RESUMES •

The purpose of a résumé is to get you a job interview. Rarely is anyone hired solely on the basis of a résumé, indeed, most employers use résumés for the initial screening of job applicants. A résumé that inspires a potential employer to interview you is one that conveys your talents and clearly demonstrates your ability to produce results that align with the particular company's goals. This is why it's so important to research your potential employers. Make certain you know to whom you are writing: learn about the company's history, its mission, needs and problems; determine the ways in which your skills can contribute to the company's success; and finally, ascertain the name and title of the person in charge of hiring (which is not always the personnel administrator).

Your cover letter is an integral part of your résumé packet. This is where you build rapport. Keep your tone friendly and use terminology that's appropriate to your field. Open your letter with something you find interesting about the company. Then inform them as to how you can be of direct benefit to the company. Close your letter by requesting an interview.

In the healing arts field, your résumé will most likely be very different from the traditional ones, where the focus on such a résumé is demonstrating results, and that may be difficult for you to do. It is important to think of your résumé not in terms of a biography, but as a prospectus for your future.

The two major types of résumés are chronological and functional. The chronological résumé is used when you want to emphasize a good work history that is directly related to your desired job. The functional résumé is used when you want to emphasize your talents, abilities and potential — not your work history. In most instances healing arts practitioners use more of a functional résumé or sometimes even just a targeted personal letter.

TARGETED PERSONAL LETTER —

A targeted personal letter is appropriate when you have a specific job in mind. It is particularly valuable when you want to focus on what you can do — regardless of whether or not you've had much experience or training. You must determine the type of job you want and specify it up front with a title (e.g., Spa Coordinator, Massage Therapist, Staff Counselor, Speech Therapist), and possibly include a short description if the title does not fully convey the job description.

As with a cover letter, the first thing to do is develop rapport. Then discuss your desired job position and give a concise, dynamic summary of your experience, capabilities and achievements that directly relate to the targeted job. You may want to include specific work history and education, but keep the focus on what you have to offer. Close the letter by suggesting a time to get together. Type this on letterhead stationery and keep the length to one page.

⌐CAL RESUME FORMAT —

⌐nd phone. Centered at top of the page.

⌐ted, name of school, degree(s), certification(s) and any awards or honors.
⌐s within the past few years, it should be the first thing listed after the
⌐ otherwise put it at the bottom.

WORK EXPERIENCE

Start with your present or most recent job. It isn't necessary to give the month and day, just the year. List your employer, job title and a brief description of your duties. Emphasize your major accomplishments and abilities. You don't have to list each position change within a company.

PERSONAL

This is optional. Only include information you feel is valuable in getting you the job.

FUNCTIONAL RESUME FORMAT —

HEADING

Name, address and phone. Centered at top of the page.

FUNCTION

List your strongest abilities or accomplishments in four or five separate paragraphs — put them in order of relevance to desired job. Have a major headline for each paragraph (e.g., Sports Psychology or Staff Management).

EDUCATION

Put at bottom unless it was within three years.

WORK EXPERIENCE

(Optional). List a brief summary at the bottom of the page. Include dates, employers and titles.

PERSONAL

Again, this is optional.

A résumé is a useful tool for promotion, even if you own your own business. If nothing else, the process of developing your résumé clarifies your strengths and reinforces your self-esteem. Before you actually prepare a résumé, I recommend that you read a book on résumés. It may give you many useful ideas and insights, and can suggest attractive and appropriate layout styles.

• FIRST IMPRESSIONS AND YOUR INTRODUCTION •

As a healing arts practitioner your ability to introduce yourself well greatly impacts your success. The current studies claim that you only have between 4 and 20 seconds to make that vital first impression. Frequently people turn off many potential clients because they don't present themselves positively and professionally. They don't take the time to develop any type of introduction, let alone a powerful one. Since this field thrives on word-of-mouth promotion, you must be able to inspire others by the way you introduce yourself.

The elements of a first impression include characteristics such as: Your appearance, facial expressions, body language, what you say, what's not said, your ability to gain rapport, your energy level and the actual message (in this situation — your introduction). An incredible amount of information and judgment occur in an extremely short period of time.

Do your best not to prejudge yourself or your audience (whether one person or one thousand). This prejudice directly effects your presentation and can substantially alter your first impression. Focus on building rapport. Your confidence in yourself and comfort with the topic will ease any nervousness.

One of the best methods to build your confidence is to have a prepared and well-rehearsed dynamic introduction. When you aren't worrying over what to say, you can focus on being with the people with whom you are talking. Actually, it is wise to have several introductions in your repertoire. The advantage is this: you may want to vary what you say and how you say it depending on the time parameters and the audience. Your introduction will differ if you are talking directly with one person rather than a group. Most likely you will use different terminology when you are talking to a group of your peers rather than a business group or even a mixed group.

In most networking groups you are only allotted 30 seconds or less to introduce yourself. Without a prepared introduction, you probably will only say a small portion of what you wish to convey. Yet 20 seconds is ample time if your basic introduction is clear, concise and engaging.

I recommend having a memorized 20 second and 30 second introduction. I also advocate designing a one minute and a five minute presentation in which you memorize your opening and closing lines, and have a clear outline of the salient points you wish to cover. Conversely, I highly discourage memorizing any presentation that is over 30 seconds in length, since this puts too much emphasis on the words and not the relationship between you and your audience. Another problem with a memorized speech is that if you forget a word or someone asks you a question, you may get totally thrown off track and not be able to gracefully recover.

SAMPLE INTRODUCTIONS —

"Hello, I am Mary Smith. I am a licensed massage therapist, specializing in prenatal massage. The work I do with pregnant women assists them in increasing circulation, reducing edema, improving muscle tone and easing tension and fatigue. Make your pregnancy — or that of a friend's — much more enjoyable and comfortable by receiving regular massages. Please feel free to talk with me after the meeting. I have cards, brochures and gift certificates available at the back table".

"Hello, I am Kerry Jones and I am a chiropractor. I've been in practice since 1985 and have recently moved to Sunny Hills. My focus is on well-being and preventative care. I have an extensive background in oriental philosophy and incorporate that into my approach. Please call me if you are interested in more information. I do not charge for an

initial consultation. I look forward to meeting with you and being able to assist you in your health and well-being".

"Do you experience a lot of stress? Is your life filled with activities — career, family and friends? Are you involved in a fitness program? If you answered yes to any of these questions, you probably experience some form of physical discomfort — be it muscular aches and pain, fatigue or even tension headaches. Massage therapy can help reduce stress, improve circulation, ease tension and improve muscle tone. I am Randy Adams and I am a certified, licensed massage therapist. If you would like more information on how massage can enhance your well-being, please talk with me after the meeting".

INTRODUCTION DESIGN —

Designing your introduction needn't be a grueling experience. You can generate and refine several introductions in less than three hours. You can make it a lot more fun by getting together with several friends and all work on your introductions. The material you develop for your introduction(s) can be utilized in creating other promotional material, such as brochures and press releases.

Begin your adventure by collecting descriptive material: Informational packets on your specific area of expertise, magazine articles, brochures from other practitioners and promotional pieces on yourself. Go through this information and highlight the words and phrases that appeal to you.

Then write a detailed statement of what you do. Be certain to distinguish the features from the benefits. Features are the descriptive characteristics about your service, your background (including experience and education) and the history/changes of your profession. Benefits are the results that a client will receive by utilizing your services.

This leads to the next step, which is clarifying in writing your "differential advantage" (see Chapter Five.) The differential advantage provides the foundation of any successful marketing piece. It addresses these questions: What does your business do? What needs does your business meet? What problems does your business solve? How will your clients benefit psychologically? How does your business differ from all the other practitioners in your field? In other words, how will your clients benefit from those aspects of your practice which are your specialties, areas of expertise and excellence and offer superior advantage.

The subsequent phase is the actual writing of your introduction. First, choose a specific audience and a time frame (e.g., a business networking meeting and 30 second general introduction). Look over all of the material you have — the highlights from your sample promotional pieces, your business description and your "differential advantage" statement. Combine these to formulate your written introduction; then review it, replacing any passive words or phrasing with the dynamic, active, present tense. To alleviate the habitual use of the same language patterns and vocabulary, get out a thesaurus and discover different words (terms, statements, jargon, expressions). If you are doing this exercise with colleagues, read your introductions to each other and get feedback. Repeat this complete process for each introduction you decide to prepare.

The final step is refining your introduction. The best way to do this is to rehearse it in front of friends (ones that will be honest with you). Get their input on the content AND your delivery (see page 17). Keep practicing until you are totally comfortable with what you say and how you say it.

• PUBLIC SPEAKING •

One of the most effective ways to promote yourself is through public speaking. This can be formal, such as lecturing, teaching and giving demonstrations; or it can be informal as in introducing yourself at a networking event. The following material covers the principles of public speaking, elucidates the steps involved in preparing a powerful presentation and provides an overview of the fundamentals of delivery.

PUBLIC SPEAKING COMPONENTS —

Public speaking is comprised of six major components: your internal state, your external behaviors, the internal state of your audience, the external behaviors of the audience, the situational format and the cultural requirements. These six elements are dynamic and continuously interact. They provide you with feedback and clues for necessary adjustments.

THE INTERNAL STATE CONTAINS SUCH FACTORS AS:

- Confidence

- Degree and type of self-talk

- Clarity of purpose

- Flexibility

- Needs

- Expectations

- Perceptions

EXTERNAL BEHAVIORS ARE THE OBSERVABLE COMPONENTS:

- Appearance

- Vocal style

- Body language

- What's said and what isn't said

- The amount and type of interaction

- Effective management of the physical environment

THE SITUATIONAL FORMAT reflects your design parameters. For example, does the presentation take place in a meeting format, a small group, a large group or one-on-one? Is this done over the radio, telephone, in person or is it done via video? Situational format is the "how" your initial contact will be structured.

THE CULTURAL ELEMENT is the "where" it will take place. Definite norms for success exist within the cultural format. For instance, you may be speaking to a small group, and the parameters for success will depend on the particular place and/or the specific audience. Is this small group meeting in a corporate setting, an educational setting or in a social setting? Are you meeting with your peers, with potential clients/employers, with athletes or with business executives. Each of these groups has distinct and often unspoken norms governing the ways which communication is expected to occur.

PRESENTATION PREPARATION —

DETERMINING PRESENTATION PURPOSE

The first step in the process of preparing a presentation is determining your purpose and intended results. In most instances, your presentation will be either informative or persuasive. In other words, do you want your audience mainly to gain understanding or do you want them to set up an appointment with you? Some presentations may have elements of both, but they still need to have one purpose.

In an informative presentation the message is subject-oriented and it's not critical that the audience accepts the topic. The objective is to disseminate information. Focus the design of your presentation in a clear and concise manner. In a persuasive presentation the message is oriented to the audience and it's vital to determine the audience's belief and acceptance level. The objective is for the audience to agree with you or decide to utilize your services. Focus on building rapport, involving the audience and fulfilling their needs.

LISTENER ANALYSIS AND ADAPTATION

The next, and quite possibly pivotal, step to any presentation is to analyze your audience. Gather as much information as possible about your potential listeners. The more you can learn about the target audience, the better able you will be to prepare for and manage your presentation.

Some of the factors to consider are: the number of people attending, the gender ratio, the age range, the informational needs, the occupations of the people in the audience, their educational and experiential background, the culture of the group, the audience's purpose for attending, their expectations and values, their format preferences, the time parameters, and the listeners' attitudes about you, your profession and your topic.

After you've done your research, you need to determine how you will make appropriate adaptations. You may want to modify the physical space, create visual aids, alter your behavioral style (voice, body language, appearance and dress), or restructure your presentation design in terms of organization, content, language and use of examples.

People like to feel that they are being talked with directly — even if they are part of a large group. Some of the techniques for involving your audience are asking a rhetorical question, having the audience participate in an activity or visualization exercise, referring to an individual or the group, requesting feedback and giving a demonstration.

The time spent tailoring a presentation for a particular audience always pays off. Use the information obtained during your analysis to design your presentation specifically for the targeted listener. Unfortunately, you may not always be able to ascertain much of this information ahead of time. That is why you must be somewhat flexible in your presentation design and pay attention to the feedback (particularly non-verbal) that you get from your audience. As you might expect, all this takes practice and experience.

MESSAGE DESIGN

The next stage is the actual design of the message. A message has three major components: the introduction, the body and the conclusion. You can enhance the effectiveness of your presentations by making your message easy to understand, powerful in impact and simple in design. Emphasis should be placed on a logical flow from one point to the next.

THE INTRODUCTION

Grab the attention of your audience and establish rapport. State the purpose of your message and provide direction for the rest of the presentation.

- Preview

- Story or Illustration

- Statement of Central Idea

- Demonstration or Example

- Rhetorical Question or Specific Question

- Testimonial or Quotation

- Opinion, Observation or Statistic

THE BODY

State each key point, intensify with subpoints and provide information to support or illustrate the points. Make clear transitions between points.

- Topical Format

    — advantages/disadvantages

    — problem/solution

    — assets/liabilities

    — function/procedure

- Chronological Format

- Cause & Effect Format

- Spatial Format

- Problem-Solving Format

- Reactionary Format

THE CONCLUSION

Briefly restate the central idea and main points. Make conclusions and recommendations. End with a final comment.

- Motivational

- Key Point Highlight

- Answer Opening Question

- Inspirational

In message design, the more customary introductions are stating a central idea, asking a question and previewing the presentation. The body is typically focused on a single point with information or evidence to support the premise. The conclusion is usually (although not always) tied to the introduction — restating the central idea, answering the opening question or calling the audience to action and summarizing the presentation. When you prepare your presentation, write out your introduction and conclusion word-for-word and memorize them. It is best to only create an outline for the body, otherwise when you are giving the presentation if you forget one word or someone asks you a question, you may totally lose your train of thought. The following are abbreviated examples of message design using the above three different introductions and conclusions.

1. *"In terms of your overall health, it's important that you consider using alternative health care practitioners. Two of the main reasons why are that they take the whole person into consideration and you play an active part in the healing process.... So, as you can see, healing arts practitioners are an important part in health enhancement. "*

2. *"How many of you have ever been to a healing arts practitioner? Healing arts practitioners are a wonderful alternative to the traditional medical view of health.... Pick up your free directory of healing arts practitioners before you leave and use their services."*

3. *"Tonight we will discuss the five major reasons why it's vital to include healing arts practitioners in your health program. The first reason is that they take the whole person into consideration: the mental, physical, emotional and spiritual aspects.... Tonight we have discussed the five major reasons for including healing arts practitioners in your health program: They take the whole person into consideration, they...."*

REFINING YOUR PRESENTATION —

After you have completed the basic design of your message, the next step is to refine your presentation. Refer to your listener analysis. Think about what types of demonstrations or visual aids you could use to enhance your presentation. Practice your presentation until you are comfortable with the content. Then rehearse it in front of a friend who will give you honest feedback on the content and delivery (see following page), record it (preferably on video but at least on audio tape), critique yourself, make any necessary changes, practice some more and repeat the whole process until you feel more at ease.

A myth exists that good public speakers do not get nervous. Everyone gets nervous! The difference between a seasoned speaker and a novice is that the seasoned speaker knows how to manage his/her nervousness by using that energy to enhance the presentation.

DELIVERY —

Approximately 55% of your presentation impact comes from your non-verbal communications, 35% from your voice and 10% from the actual content. Yet most people spend the majority of their preparation on the content. Power and presence are established through the mastery of body language while the energy in your voice conveys your sincerity. In order to truly refine your delivery, it's essential that you be videotaped. If you have a visual impairment, then get someone to coach you. Quite often, we are unaware of our mannerisms, gestures, speech patterns and vocal quirks. And seeing yourself on videotape may be the only way you ever discover them. The following list covers the basic elements of delivery.

APPEARANCE: Be dressed appropriately and be well-groomed. Keep all of your jewelry and accessories to a minimum.

POSTURE: Sit or stand in an erect yet relaxed position.

MOVEMENT: Make movements reinforce what you are saying and involve your audience. Avoid pacing, shuffling and any erratic motions.

POSITION: Place yourself so that you can see your entire audience. Start far enough back so that you can move toward the audience.

GESTURES: Make certain your gestures are smooth and precise. Use them to reinforce your message. Avoid nervous habits.

FACIAL EXPRESSIONS: Use your head and face to accentuate your message and build rapport. Avoid excessive nodding.

EYE CONTACT: Slowly scan your audience, then maintain direct eye contact with several select individuals.

BREATHING: Keep your shoulders relaxed and breathe into your diaphragm.

TEMPO: Be certain to keep a smooth flow in your rate of speech.

RHYTHM: Occasionally vary your pattern of speech.

ARTICULATION: Express sounds and words distinctly and clearly.

VITALITY: Keep your energy level high. Be certain that you don't fade out.

PROJECTION: Learn how to modify your vocal volume.

PURPOSEFUL PAUSE: Pause for emphasis, anticipation or reflection.

HIGHLIGHT: Accentuate key words or phrases.

Remember, it takes a while to build up public speaking skills. Ultimately, it's wise to take a seminar in presentation skills or join a speaking group so you can fully develop your vocal qualities, body language and overall speaking abilities.

CHAPTER FOUR

PRACTICE MANAGEMENT

PRACTICE MANAGEMENT

• MANAGING YOUR BUSINESS •

Effective management of a business takes commitment and creativity. One of the strangest phenomena is that most corporations spend too much time in planning and managing (thus not enough "doing"), while most small businesses invest little or no time in planning and managing themselves (thus work from a reactive instead of proactive state).

Success strategies for managing a business include staying balanced, aligning your personal growth with your business, having a written business plan, developing excellent self management skills, managing finances (including forecasting, accurate bookkeeping and cash flow management), writing goals, creating strategic plans of action, having a business support system, networking, refining communication skills, periodically reviewing all of your goals and plans and most important of all — making sure you have fun!

This chapter on practice management focuses on providing you with practical information, definitions, forms and techniques to enhance your effectiveness in the actual day-to-day running of your business.

The first section covers the basic elements of business start-up such as: choosing a name, financing, selecting a location, licensing and insurance coverage. You will find it beneficial to review this segment even if you have been in business a while. The next section explores the benefits and limitations of a sole practice, partnership and an association. Immediately following, is information on how to ascertain whether or not an independent contractor is actually an employee. Then there's an overview on the ways to build an effective relationship with your clerical staff. Next are methods to determine your fee structure. The rest of this section covers the paperwork aspects of practice management such as: client files, bookkeeping, taxes, policy and procedure manuals and insurance billing.

I do not advocate creating a paperwork jungle. Simpler is usually better. Keep in mind that recordkeeping need not be a horrendous chore. Once you have set up appropriate filing systems and procedures for documentation, you will find that it takes very little effort to keep your records current.

Maintaining accurate and up-to-date records is crucial to any business. It is important to be able to quickly ascertain the status of your finances as well as the condition of any given client.

Take the time to formulate your policies and create a written policy and procedure manual: even if you are the only person in your business. By going through this process, you may discover conflicts or potential risky situations, and thus be able to address and resolve these issues before they actually arise. Also, if you decide to expand your practice and hire staff (or bring in an associate), the transition will be easier if the operational guidelines are already established.

Practice management is the area most people neglect or avoid, yet it can mean the difference between having a smooth, joyful business and one that's operated from a crisis management perspective.

• BUSINESS START-UP •

Proper business start-up makes a tremendous difference in your practice. If you are aware of the local and federal requirements of your particular business (e.g., zoning, licensing, federal identification number, etc.), then you can make appropriate choices and structure your business (before you even open your doors) so that you will be in compliance of these rules and regulations.

"It's never too late to start over" is a common saying, although one not normally associated with business. Yet, in many ways, you really can "start over" regardless of how long you have been in practice. Although it can be more difficult to make changes after the fact, it's not impossible.

FINANCING —

Financing your business (be it for start-up or expansion) can be frustrating. Even though a lot of venture capital is available, it's extremely difficult to procure investment money for a service business. Be extremely wary of any company that guarantees (for an up-front fee) to find you venture capital. There are a lot of scam operations being perpetrated against the naive small business owner. To find reputable sources of funding, check out the resource guides at your local Small Business Administration office.

A bank may be willing to give you a loan, but it will usually be based upon your assets. Applying for a loan (or venture investment) takes a lot of work: research, correspondence, proposals, refining your business plan — including financial statements and cash flow forecasts (they want to see numbers) and putting together an impressive presentation.

Most small business owners finance their company with money from personal savings or through loans from close friends and relatives. If you decide to borrow money from friends or family, treat them with the same consideration that you would give to a formal lending institution. Make an official presentation and submit a loan proposal and a business plan. Clearly delineate the terms of the loan and the repayment schedule. We've all heard the horror stories about borrowing money from loved ones, but if you do it correctly and set your boundaries, it can be a wonderful experience — one in which everyone benefits personally and financially.

BUSINESS NAME —

Choosing an appropriate name for your business takes some contemplation. Most healing arts practitioners are their business and thus, need to go no further. But, you may want to have a separate business identity, particularly if you have a group practice. If so, choose your name carefully and avoid anything gimmicky. Select a name that conveys the essence of your business (see Chapter Five) in a manner that inspires people to find out more about your services.

If you designate a business name other than your legal personal name, you must file a Fictitious Name Statement. This is often referred to as a DBA (Doing Business As) form. Contact your county clerk for the forms and procedures.

As a sole proprietor healing arts practitioner, you don't need an employee identification number (EIN) unless you have employees or a Keogh plan. (See IRS Publication 583 for specifics.) Otherwise, you can use your social security number. To get an EIN, file form SS-4 with your local IRS office.

LOCATION —

Appropriate site location is vital from both a marketing and an operational point of view. You want to choose a site that will attract clients, fit your business image, accommodate your business needs (and potential expansion) in terms of size and layout, is properly zoned and priced within your budget.

Office prices vary greatly depending on the actual location and the local economics. Before signing a lease, check out the going rates on other comparable office space. Comparable is the key word. Read the fine print. The quoted price might not include such things as utilities, parking, leasehold improvements (lighting, decorations and structural changes to the floors and walls), signage, etc.

Being knowledgeable of the zoning ordinances in your area can save you a lot of hassle, time and money. It is better to find out what these laws are before you start your practice or change locations. The four basic zoning classifications are residential, commercial, industrial and agricultural. Zoning laws were instituted to protect residential neighborhoods from any potential negative influences. The regulations vary greatly from city to county to state.

One of the first steps in discovering the zoning ordinances is to contact your local zoning commission. You can also talk with the Chamber of Commerce or the Business Licensing Bureau. If you want to work out of your home, you also need to refer to the property deed to see what additional restrictions might exist.

LICENSES AND PERMITS —

Business owners need to know the local, state and federal requirements that influence the starting or relocating of a business. The following list is an overview of the basic required licenses and permits, and who to contact for specific information and forms. This list doesn't cover every possible situation, as your business may have special site requirements or industry regulations.

BUSINESS LICENSE

This allows you the privilege of doing business. Contact your Business Licensing Bureau.

OCCUPATIONAL LICENSE

This allows you to work in a specific industry as long as you comply with that profession's regulations. Contact the State Agency of Consumer Affairs or the local Business Licensing Bureau.

TRANSACTION PRIVILEGE TAX LICENSE

This allows you to collect (and remit) sales tax. Contact your State Department of Revenue.

PLANNING AND ZONING PERMITS

These permits are issued after your location has been assessed and shows that the business operation conforms with area plans, has proper zoning and has adequate parking, etc. Contact your City/County Hall Planning Department.

BUILDING SAFETY PERMIT

This permit is issued after your location is inspected and is found safe for you and your clients, and complies with fire and building codes. Contact the local Fire Department.

INSURANCE COVERAGE —

Being properly insured is imperative for any small business. Discuss your specific needs with an insurance agent (or two) to determine the types and amount of insurance that is appropriate for you and your business. Don't make any assumptions about your coverage. Check your office lease thoroughly. Your leaseholder may not be responsible for providing complete coverage. Also, if you work out of your home, be certain to review your homeowner's or apartment-dweller's policy. While the standard homeowner's policy protects you from personal liability if a guest is injured at your home, it will not cover you if the visit is related to business.

You may need to have more than one insurance carrier because very few companies will offer all of the types of coverage that you desire. The major types of insurance policies are small business, liability, partnership, general liability, malpractice liability, automobile, fire and theft, personal disability, medical insurance and worker's compensation.

LIABILITY INSURANCE covers costs of injuries that occur on your property to business-related visitors. Don't assume that this is automatically covered in your office lease. Also, if you work out of your home, your homeowner's policy might not cover this either.

GENERAL LIABILITY INSURANCE covers negligence resulting in injury to clients, employees and the general public while you are on their premises.

SMALL BUSINESS INSURANCE provides umbrella coverage for business losses in terms of general liability, business interruption, errors and omissions, and product liability.

MALPRACTICE LIABILITY INSURANCE protects you from claims due to a loss incurred by your clients as a result of negligence or failure on your part to perform at a professional skill level.

AUTOMOBILE INSURANCE is very important, particularly if you use your car in your business. Be sure to carry full coverage — including disability, business interruption and loss or damage to business-related items.

FIRE AND THEFT INSURANCE covers business equipment, furniture, supplies and documents. If you work out of your home, you may need to get a rider to get adequate protection. You will most likely need a separate policy for an outside office.

PERSONAL DISABILITY INSURANCE safeguards you from loss of income if you are unable to work due to illness or injury. You are paid a certain monthly amount if you are permanently disabled or a portion if you are partially disabled (can include long term illness). This type of insurance is essential if you are the head of your household or don't have sufficient savings.

MEDICAL HEALTH INSURANCE is to help cover medical bills, particularly for complicated illnesses, injuries and hospitalization.

WORKER'S COMPENSATION is required by law if you have employees. It covers all of the costs that you as an employer would be required to pay for any injury to an employee.

PARTNERSHIP INSURANCE protects you against lawsuits arising from the actions or omissions by any of your business partners.

• SOLE PRACTICE, PARTNERSHIPS AND ASSOCIATIONS •

At some point in your practice, you may find yourself considering expanding the scope of your business and including one or more associates or even partners. Deciding whether or not to involve another person in your business and then choosing that person can be a very difficult process. Your choice can greatly impact all aspects of your life. The benefits of having an associate/partner are: it can help ease the loneliness of being self-employed, enable you to take time off and provide you with another person with whom you can brainstorm ideas and share expenses. It could also be a nightmare.

An association is when two or more people get together to share some resources and expenses, yet keep separate business identities. A partnership is when two or more people contribute assets to carry on a jointly owned business and share in the profits or losses. In order to be considered a partnership, you do not have to use the term "partners", or have a written partnership agreement or equally share ownership. The operative phrase here is "jointly owned". In most instances, healing arts practitioners tend to form associations rather than partnerships. In either case, I encourage you to read *The Partnership Book* by Clifford & Warner. This book is filled with excellent information and sample forms for developing partnership agreements that can also be adapted for association agreements.

Even though the legal and financial aspects are vastly different between a partnership and an association, the requisite self-assessment and role clarification process is the same. I strongly advocate you carefully consider any changes to your status of sole practitioner.

The first phase in making a choice of an associate/partner is clarifying your reasons for wanting to share your business (or space) with another person. For instance, are you doing this because you want to or is it mainly stemming from a financial need? It is vital that you assess your temperament to determine if it's appropriate for you to have another person involved in your business. Think about how you want to share your space and how much do you need to control it: if you are uncomfortable when things aren't done in a specific manner, then it may become difficult for you to share an office, let alone be in partnership. If you decide to go ahead with the idea, you need to be clear about the desired relationship between yourself and your potential associate/partner. Do you want this person to play an active role in your business or would you rather just have someone to share ideas and expenses. Make a list of the characteristics of your "ideal associate". Then highlight those qualities that are absolutely essential.

After you have clarified your reasons for wanting an associate/partner and have envisioned his/her qualities, it's time to conduct interviews. Your closest friends or colleagues may not be the wisest choices. Invest the time required to do this well; after all, this is someone you may be seeing day in and day out. Share with each other your dreams, goals and concerns. Some of the questions to consider are: How long do you intend to stay in this location, what kind of work schedule to you prefer to keep, what type of atmosphere do you want to have, who do you want as clients, do you ultimately want additional associates or employees and do you plan on incorporating other services or products? Look for the commonalities and possible areas of conflict. Do your businesses complement each other? Are your fee structures similar? Then discuss the ways you like to handle the logistics of your businesses. Oftentimes this seemingly unimportant aspect can ruin otherwise great associations. For example, if you like to burn incense and your associate hates it — resentment may build. Also, get to know each other's communication style and see if your personalities are compatible. For example, if you prefer a methodical approach to business and your partner tends to work best under pressure — you may be in for a tempestuous association.

If you have decided that indeed you would like to be associates or partners, the next step is to delineate — **IN WRITING** — your roles and expectations. List all of the things that are important to you in running your business. Be certain to include the following issues:

ATMOSPHERE

Agree upon the way clients are to be greeted, the layout of the waiting area, the beverages you make available, the background music and the noise level (e.g., if you do guided meditations, it might be inappropriate to share space with someone who does emotional release therapy — unless the building is suitably soundproofed).

LOGISTICS

Decide who will be responsible for paying the bills, create a budget for shared expenses (with a caveat against jointly making any major purchases unless you are indeed partners), choose who will buy the supplies and set up a cleaning schedule (be sure to clarify a mutual minimum level of acceptance).

PROMOTION

Determine what percentage of the advertising is to be done jointly, how the phone shall be listed in the phone book and the types of joint promotions you will consider.

LEVEL OF INTERACTION

Consider how often you want to have "staff" meetings, the degree and manner of mutual support and do you want to pursue a friendship in addition to being associates.

In setting up your agreements, be certain to take into consideration that people tend to gravitate toward different tasks and may become bored with particular chores, so it's wise to review, evaluate and possibly reassign your responsibilities every few months. Remember, care-givers have a tendency to neglect themselves, so don't just take on your associate's responsibilities and "take care of him/her." Be sure to communicate. It is essential to set boundaries and realize that not everything will be agreed upon and shared. It is at this point that you have to decide whether or not you can live with the compromises. But, if you do this before you become associates/partners, it will help avoid future misunderstandings and rancor. Even so, you must also decide (in advance) what you will actually do in the event of a broken agreement or irreconcilable differences.

In addition to writing your shared vision, goals, roles and expectations, I strongly encourage you to create a dissolution (or buyout) agreement. Who knows what the future holds? People's goals can change or major life-altering circumstances may occur. Make sure that you both have a realistic means to ethically and amicably part ways. If you decide to become partners (and not just associates), I highly recommend you design a full business plan (see Chapter Six) before the partnership is official. In the process of developing your business plan, you will both be compelled to evaluate your strengths and weaknesses, clarify your financial arrangements, delineate your roles, determine legal responsibilities and refine your business vision.

The final step is to have a business consultant and/or an attorney review your plans and agreements — even if you are just associates and not "partners".

• INDEPENDENT CONTRACTOR OR EMPLOYEE? •

Many practitioners find themselves in the position of wanting to expand the scope of their business and include other allied healing arts practitioners. Quite often, they bring them in as "independent contractors", when in reality they are employees.

Hiring independent contractors can seem appealing. As the business owner, you aren't required to withhold taxes; you don't have to pay worker's compensation premiums, unemployment taxes and matching social security taxes (FICA); and you don't have to provide fringe benefits such as health insurance, paid vacations, sick leave and retirement plans.

The downside to this is that if the IRS determines that your independent contractors are (or were) indeed employees, you may be required to pay fines (of up to 100% of the tax) in addition to the back income taxes and social security taxes. This can easily add up to a sizeable amount. In the eyes of the IRS, it makes no difference if you signed an agreement that states you are contracting with an independent contractor (although a written agreement is advisable).

You do not have to withhold income tax or social security tax from independent contractors. But, if you pay an independent contractor $600.00 or more during the year in the course of your trade or business, you must file a form 1099-MISC (see page 22). If you have common-law employees, you may have to withhold income tax and social security tax. You may also have to pay federal unemployment tax, worker's compensation and your share of social security on these wages.

In order to assist in your understanding of this complex topic, I am providing the following information (adapted with permission) from IRS Publication 937, Business Reporting:

> Under common-law rules, every individual who performs services subject to the will and control of an employer, as to both what must be done and how it must be done, is an employee. It does not matter that the employer allows the employee discretion and freedom of action, so long as the employer has the legal right to control both the method and the result of the services.

> Two usual characteristics of an employer-employee relationship are that the employer has the right to discharge the employee and the employer supplies the employee with tools and a place to work. (Now don't assume that you can get around this by having your "employee" provide his/her own specific supplies. Tools is a broad term that can include the equipment required in running a practice such as telephones, copiers, etc.).

> If you have an employer-employee relationship, it makes no difference how it is described. It does not matter if the employee is called an employee, associate, partner or independent contractor. It also doesn't matter how the payments are measured, made or what they are called. Nor does it matter whether the individual is employed full time or part time.

The IRS has developed the following list of twenty factors that they use to determine the status of employee or independent contractor. The degree of importance of each factor varies according to the profession and the conditions in which the services are performed. The most important factor is control. If the business owner has the right to control how and when a person works, then that person is most likely to be considered an employee.

AN INDIVIDUAL IS LIKELY TO BE CONSIDERED AN EMPLOYEE IF S/HE:

1. Is required to comply with company instructions about when, where and how to work.

2. Has been trained by the company to perform services in a particular manner.

3. Has his/her services integrated into the company's operations because the services are critical to the success of the business.

4. Must render services personally.

5. Utilizes assistants provided by the company.

6. Has an ongoing, continuing relationship with the company.

7. Has set work hours established by the employer.

8. Is required to work the equivalent of full time.

9. Works on the company's designated premise.

10. Must perform services in the order or sequence determined by the employer.

11. Must submit regular progress reports.

12. Is paid in regular intervals such as by the hour, week or month.

13. Is reimbursed for all business and travel expenses.

14. Uses tools and materials furnished by the employer.

15. Has no significant investment in the facilities that are used.

16. Has no risk of loss.

17. Works for only one person or company.

18. Does not offer services to the general public.

19. Can be discharged by the company.

20. Can terminate the relationship without incurring liability.

Realize that you can still qualify an individual as an independent contractor even if some of these factors are present in your working relationship. The key elements in this industry involve who regulates the type of work and how, where and when it's done; who determines the fee structure; who receives the money from the client; who provides the equipment and supplies; who pays for the client-related expenses; and who generates the clientele.

The two most viable ways to minimize the risk of your independent contractor being reclassified as an employee is to make certain that this person has multiple sources of income or lease him/her from a third-party agency. When it comes to augmenting your staff, be very careful how you classify these people. Just calling someone an independent contractor doesn't make it so. The risks you take are usually not worth the ostensible benefits. If in doubt, you can have the IRS determine whether a worker is an employee by filing Form SS-8.

In general, it's wise to consider an individual as an employee until you can prove otherwise.

• CLERICAL SUPPORT STAFF •

Your clerical support staff is one of the quintessential operational assets of any small business. They are often the first encounter a potential client has with your business. In those first few minutes (as well as in the continuing relationship with established clients — see Chapter Five), your clerical support staff establishes the persona of your business, its image and philosophy. Therefore, having the right type of person with the proper skills for your particular job requirements and client service is critical.

The first step is to identify what type of support you need. What are the job duties? Are you looking for a receptionist, secretary, bookkeeper, administrative assistant or operations manager? Each type of position has differing job duties and responsibilities. They may appear to be basically the same; however, they are not. You can confuse yourself and the employee by misunderstanding the differences or defining them poorly in the job description. Duties are those assigned work tasks in a given job such as typing, filing, answering the phones, taking messages, etc. Responsibilities are those tasks that the position is accountable for (e.g., producing monthly reports, filing insurance claims, analyzing data, maintaining databases, taking messages correctly, accurately proofreading, etc.). In order to screen your candidates, interview effectively and hire intelligently, the position must be specified clearly and succinctly. You need to determine whether the position will be part-time or full-time; what hours you require; and the wage rate according to the demands of the position and the skill level required.

Not only is it important to be specific about the job duties and responsibilities, you need to determine what personality will best suit you and your business. Each individual, as well as each business, has a certain personality. In order to have the optimum in working harmony and best service to your clients, you need to decide what kind of personality you can work "with" well and is appropriate for the type of business you have. Keep in mind that your clerical support personnel is most likely the first encounter your clients have with your business. That interaction can influence whether or not a client returns. Your established clients are also important and the relationship your clerical support establishes with them is vital. Clients, especially in the healing arts practice, need the feeling of trust, security, welcome and caring that the clerical support staff should provide. Not only does your support staff need to efficiently take care of the "mechanics" of the position, they need to be mindful of projecting an honest sense of "caring" toward your clients. There are many little things that can be done with each client which promotes your business' persona such as:

- Knowing your client's name.

- Asking how s/he is doing.

- Having a sympathetic ear (listening to those grumbles and complaints and understanding how the client is feeling).

- Asking if there is anything else that can be done for him/her.

- Wishing him/her a good day.

- Being sensitive to and paying special attention to their demeanor: "You look tired today, hope you're feeling better." "You look terrific today, full of energy."

- Even a compliment on an attractive outfit, hair cut, etc. brings goodwill.

Once you have established the position's duties, responsibilities and the personality you need to project the persona of your business, you must design your interview questions in order to ascertain the most information about your candidates and whether they will fit into the mold you have established for the job. Consider the following (true) story: A manager had gone through five secretaries in one year. She finally determined that obviously something was wrong, otherwise, why would five different secretaries quit within a one year period? The manager established that she needed to know what would make an individual person quit. Hence, in the interview, one of the of the questions she asked was simply, "What would make you quit a job?" She also established a certain "personality" that she knew was needed in order to work together effectively and harmoniously. So, one of the other questions became, "Are you a beautiful person inside?"

Therefore, by identifying your position well and designing your interview effectively, you enable yourself to choose the best possible support staff. Not just for yourself and your business persona, but for those you serve.

Once you have hired that individual person, your job is not done. As a manager/supervisor you are responsible for literally "supporting" your support staff. Simply establishing the position and hiring a person to fill it isn't the end, it's the beginning of a working "relationship". One of the most important concepts to grasp is that you are working "with" someone. This establishes a sense of team work and camaraderie. Remember, you will be working with this individual at least eight hours a day, five days a week. Quality intercommunication is essential. If issues arise regarding job performance, they need to be handled diplomatically and quickly.

Be certain to listen to your staff; they are the ones who deal with daily tasks and generally have some very creative, imaginative and efficient methods of conducting their work. Never underestimate your staff. They may have some surprising abilities that when allowed to come forth will be an asset to your business. They may not have a college degree or may not be versed in the intricacies of your profession, but don't insult their intelligence.

It is also important to allow individual autonomy and not be over-controlling. Give your staff the authority to make decisions. Make certain they understand your policies and know when they can determine the proper action (and when they must first confer with you). It is okay to oversee your staff and review their actions, but don't monitor their every move.

Institute annual performance reviews which not only evaluate job performance, but also establish goals and objectives for the coming year. Review the position duties and responsibilities and make adjustments according to the changing needs of your office operations. Make this performance review a two way communication. Ask your staff to clarify:

1. Their perception of their duties and responsibilities.

2. What contributions have they made to the position other than the mechanics of the job?

3. What goals and objectives do they have for the coming year?

4. What additional seminars, lectures or outside activities would they like to participate in — relative to their position and enhanced job knowledge and performance?

Answer these questions from your perspective and then sit down together to review them. This allows each of you to jointly assess the previous year, while lessening the opportunity for misunderstanding and poor communication about each of your expectations and needs.

Included in this performance evaluation should be an objective review of performance (e.g., Quality of Work, Quantity of Work, Communication, Timeliness, etc.).

A well designed performance evaluation can be used as an excellent management tool promoting effective and clear communication and establishing a sense of teamwork to promote a satisfying working relationship.

Don't wait until the end of the coming year to informally discuss progress and concerns. Conduct informal reviews quarterly, if not monthly. This provides an occasion for you to affirm exceptional performance, correct minor difficulties before they become major problems and initiate changes in operational needs in a timely manner. It also allows your staff the opportunity to discuss those matters of concern they may have in their working relationship with you or your clients.

In addition to reviews, you need to hold staff meetings. These should be at least once per month and preferably once per week. These meetings serve to build camaraderie as well as providing a forum to discuss problems, learn new skills, brainstorm ideas and set goals.

Unfortunately, in any business, you will find the "Jobs That Nobody Wants To Do" — the tasks that are either boring, unpleasant or difficult to accomplish. It is not uncommon for resentments to arise around these noxious tasks. As a manager, you need to find a way to balance these duties among your staff. This can be difficult when you only have one employee or if you are the only person in your business. If you're lucky, you will find someone who loves to do those tasks that everyone else hates. Alas, these people tend to be rare. So, the next best option is to hold a staff meeting and brainstorm ideas for dealing with these tasks. Conducting brainstorming sessions and including your staff in some of the decision making processes will make them feel as though they are part of a team — and when people feel that they are working as a team, they will be less apt to feel resentful over having to do those "awful" assignments.

One of the outcomes of a brainstorming session might be a change in the company's operations and procedures. Sometimes a slight alteration in the execution of a task can alleviate the dread associated with doing it. Frequently, tasks can be simplified or even eliminated. Changes don't occur very often because people rarely take the time to evaluate policies, procedures and goals. Another outcome of the brainstorming session may be that the staff decides to rotate these unpleasant tasks. Whatever the results of this session are, it's imperative that you follow through and monitor the progress.

The net results in the proper management of your clerical support staff are the optimum in working harmony, efficiency in working capacity, the building of good working relations with your staff, establishing goodwill with your clients and a bottom line that shows black.

• SETTING YOUR FEES •

Setting an appropriate fee structure (and increase strategy) is necessary in any business. No matter which method you choose for determining your rates, be certain that your fee structure promotes credibility.

Four major strategies exist for determining fees:

1. You can set a very high price, thus targeting a small percentage of the population. This usually only works if your service is innovative, in demand and has no competition.

2. A competitive pricing strategy is simply setting your price with the going rate for the industry.

3. If you want to get a larger share of the market, your strategy might be to set a significantly lower fee than the standard rate.

4. Finally, if you want to break into a new market, your strategy may include offering introductory (reduced or two-for-one) rates for a limited time, package deals or a sliding scale. Just beware of the ongoing sale syndrome.

Before you finalize your fee structure, carefully consider all of the costs involved in running your business. This includes your fixed costs such as rent, utilities, phone, equipment, loan payments, maintenance, insurance, licenses, advertising and staffing, as well as the amenities that vary depending on the number and type of clients. These more nebulous amenities include providing free samples and educational materials, taxes, supplies, promotional costs and your time: keeping client records, networking, planning, holding extended business hours, travelling, practice management, continuing your education and consultations.

The chart on the next page illustrates how to determine your fees. It is based on a 40 hour work week, which leaves a maximum of 25 billable hours per week. Since overhead varies greatly from one business to another, it's not included in this breakdown.

For example, let's say that you want to earn $35,000.00 this year. If you plan on working 50% (billing 12.5 hours per week), then you need to charge $54.00 per hour. If you think you will be able to work 90% (bill 22.5 hours per week), then you only need to charge $30.00 per hour. BUT, you also must include the costs in running your business. (Refer to your Cash Flow Forecast in Chapter Six).

Imagine that your fixed costs are $10,000.00 per year plus $6.00 per client. So, at a 50% workload, you need to cover $35,000.00 income, $10,000.00 fixed expenses, and $3,900.00 per client cost (650 people), which equals $48,900.00. Now, look at the chart and you will find that to bring in gross revenues of $50,000.00, you need to charge approximately $76.00 per hour.

Yet, if you plan on billing 90%, then you need to cover $35,000.00 income, $10,000.00 fixed expenses, and $7,020.00 per client (1170 people) cost, which equals $52,020.00. Check the chart and you will discover that you will only need to charge about $39.00 per hour.

TIME/INCOME FACTOR ANALYSIS

One Year	= 365 days	-	104 days (weekends)
	= 261 days	-	8 days (holidays)
	= 253 days	-	10 days (health)
	= 243 days	-	10 days (vacation)
	= 233 days	x	8 hours per day
	= 1,864 hours per year		
	- 30% (promotion, operations, professional development)		
	= approximately 1300 hours		
	= approximately 25 billable hours per week		

Annual Income*	50% 12.5 hrs/week (650 hrs)	70% 17.5 hrs/week (910 hrs)	90% 22.5 hrs/week (1170 hrs)	100% 25 hrs/week (1300 hrs)
$25,000	38.50	27.50	21.50	19.25
$30,000	46.00	33.00	25.75	23.00
$35,000	54.00	38.50	30.00	27.00
$40,000	61.50	44.00	34.00	31.00
$50,000	77.00	55.00	42.75	38.50
$60,000	92.00	66.00	51.25	46.00
$75,000	115.50	82.50	64.00	58.00
$100,000	154.00	110.00	85.50	77.00

* Does not include allowance for overhead and taxes

This chart can have an unsettling effect. You may be wondering how you can possibly earn the income you desire while charging a fair and equitable price. Several possibilities exist for increasing your income potential. First of all, you can increase the number of billable weekly hours by working more than 40 hours per week (which is not uncommon with small business owners). Another alternative is to reduce your overhead costs — but be certain you do this in such a way that your clients don't experience a decrease in benefits. You can also diversify your practice by selling products, subcontracting work (or hiring other practitioners to work for you) and leading seminars, etc. Finally, one of the most viable options is to delegate some of your business activities, which frees you to increase the number of hours of direct client contact.

When you have determined that you must raise your fees, be certain the increase is appropriate. You will probably lose credibility (and clients) if you raise your rates more than once per year. Do a one year financial forecast. Ascertain the amount of money you need to charge per session should you experience no growth in your business. Raise your fees accordingly, with a caveat against an increase of greater than fifteen percent.

Inform your clients of your rate changes at least two weeks in advance. Springing a higher charge on them at the last moment (particularly right AFTER a session) is very disrespectful. If you offer series discounts, promote goodwill by allowing your clients the opportunity to sign up for a series at the "old" rates. Of course, they need to make this commitment before the new fee structure goes into effect.

Determining your appropriate fee structure involves more than simply deciding what you want to charge per hour. You have to balance your desired income and requisite expenses with what's realistic. Your fees must be fair and instill trust. Even if you are considered to be the best practitioner in your field, it's futile to charge more than what the market will bear. Just because you desire a specific income level and feel you deserve to charge a certain rate, doesn't necessarily mean that people will pay it. So, choose your market(s) carefully and then strategize your fee structure. Keep in mind that raising your hourly rates is not the only way to increase your income.

• CLIENT FILES •

Client files serve two major purposes. The first purpose has to do with record-keeping and the Internal Revenue Service. When you are in a service industry, basically the only way you can document your "work" is to have client files. The second major purpose for maintaining files is to keep you well informed of your client's needs. It is not wise to rely only upon your memory for details regarding your client's history and treatment plan. The rudimentary information to include in each file is the client's name, address, phone number, medical history, current medication, reason(s) for using your services, session dates and amounts paid.

Many types of client files have been developed over the years. You may want to use those forms, adapt them or customize one for your own specific needs. If you are a medical professional or bill insurance companies, you must use the recognized procedures and appropriate codes. The standard charting method in the medical field is called **S.O.A.P.** (an acronym for **S**ubjective, **O**bjective, **A**ssessment and **P**lan). The following is a brief definition of **S.O.A.P**:

SUBJECTIVE

A description of the symptoms and complaints discussed by the client (or the referring primary health care provider) that is inscribed using the patient's own words.

OBJECTIVE

An account of the actual treatment administered and your observations.

ASSESSMENT

A record of the analysis of the information, which may include the patient's goals as well as response to treatment.

PLAN

A list of recommended action.

Regardless of the type of forms you use, accurate record-keeping is essential. Whenever you see a client for the first time, be sure to do an intake interview. After the client has completed filling out any initial paperwork, review it with him/her. People don't always read things thoroughly, misunderstand questions, don't fit multiple choice responses or forget to write down details that could influence the treatment plan.

Set it up so that your client files are useful. Make notes after each session (it can even be a visual record, such as shading a section of a drawing), include anything unexpected that may have happened during the session, things you want to follow up on, specific techniques you want to include next time and anything else that you feel is important to remember.

Review your files immediately before you work with each client. This will assist you in being more focused with all of your clients. It can really destroy a client's trust and respect in you if you don't "remember" what occurred during his/her last session, (even though you may have seen thirty other people since then). So, it is better to be prepared. Also, before each session, ask the client if there are any changes or additions that need to be included on the form.

You must decide what purpose your client files are going to serve and then choose the appropriate forms. You may want to know personal information such as a client's birthday, family details (e.g., names of spouse/significant other and children) or the types of personal growth work the client has done. It is also helpful to know how they found out about you, so you can determine where to focus your advertising.

As you and your needs change, you most likely will modify the forms you use. Some practitioners also include an explanation of the range/variety of services and techniques they offer and list some of the benefits of their services on the top of their intake forms. Other practitioners also incorporate a type of disclaimer. For example, many massage therapists put a statement that massage is clearly non-sexual.

You will find some samples of client file forms in Appendix A. Please use them or adapt them for your specific needs.

• BOOKKEEPING •

All too often healing arts professionals have a limited financial background and view bookkeeping as an evil chore or an arcane art to deaden the psyche. Since most people will do almost anything to avoid chores, many practitioners do not keep accurate records, if they keep records at all. Thus, they tend to miss numerous legitimate tax deductions. Keeping records is a habit that must be developed. It is highly recommended that you consult with a bookkeeper or an accountant when setting up your books and most definitely when it's time to fill out your tax returns. The tax laws are complex and seem to change every other week. The following information is provided to assist you in developing your bookkeeping system. It has been streamlined as much as possible.

BASIC DO'S AND DON'TS —

DON'T:

1. Throw away any business related receipt
2. Pay bills until they are due — unless you receive a discount for early payment

DO:

1. Have a separate business checking account
2. Keep records for at least 7 years
   A. Receipts
   B. Bank statements
   C. Copies of tax returns
   D. Ledger sheets
      • Income Received: Record all pertinent information on checks received — client name, check number, amount, date and type of income. Keep a separate sheet for barter income.
      • Check Disbursements
      • Cash Disbursements
      • Accounts Receivable
      • Summaries
      • Profit & Loss Statements
3. Keep lists of inventory, equipment & furniture
4. Maintain client files
5. Make cash flow projections
6. Keep mileage logs
7. Maintain daily records
   A. Keep an appointment book/diary
   B. List all incidental cash expenses (e.g., mineral water while waiting for a client... it adds up) in a daily diary and then record on a cash disbursement ledger sheet (or petty cash fund sheet).
   C. Keep activity tracking sheets
8. Prepare monthly bank reconciliations

Maintaining accurate records is vital for any small business. All too often, the checkbook doesn't give an accurate account of the business's financial standing. It is not necessary to spend a fortune on a bookkeeping system. Sometimes simple columnar sheets from an office supply store will suffice — or use sample ledger sheets from Appendix A. Don't make bookkeeping more complicated than it needs to be.

Below and on the following pages, you will find definitions of accounting terms and filled-in examples of an income journal sheet, a disbursement journal sheet, a cash flow projection sheet and a listing of common business expenses. Blank copies of these forms along with a mileage record and a bank reconciliation form can be found in Appendix A. Please use them as guidelines for creating your own bookkeeping system.

ACCOUNTING DEFINITIONS —

ASSETS
The total resources (current, fixed or other) of the sole practitioner or business — tangible and intangible. Assets may include cash in the bank, goodwill, accounts receivable and equipment.

LIABILITIES
Current and long term debts of the practitioner or business. Liabilities may include accounts payable, long term debts, (e.g., a car loan), payroll taxes and credit card balances.

ACCOUNTS RECEIVABLE
The amounts owed to you by another person or business.

ACCOUNTS PAYABLE
The amounts you owe another person or business.

CAPITAL
Essentially it is the net worth of a business — the difference between the assets and the liabilities.

CAPITAL ACCOUNT
The total money invested by the owner.

JOURNAL
A book of original entry for recording complete information on all transactions (e.g., Monthly Receipts/Income Journal and Monthly Expense Disbursements Journal).

LEDGER
Summary sheets — final entry.

SUB-LEDGERS
Where Accounts Receivable and Accounts Payable are recorded.

CREDITS
Entries made on the right side of an account. Credits reduce Asset Account and Expense Account, and increase Liability, Capital and Income Accounts.

DEBITS
Entries made on the left side of an account. Debits increase Asset and Expense Accounts, and reduce Liability, Capital and Income Accounts.

DRAWING ACCOUNT
As the owner of your business, you may withdraw cash for personal use. It is similar to a salary, except that you don't take out withholding taxes (that is why you pay self-employment taxes). Withdrawals can reduce the owner's equity.

PETTY CASH FUND
Cash on hand to pay for incidental expenses. Put a voucher in the petty cash drawer and record each transaction. Do not put cash received from a client into the petty cash fund. When the fund is low, write a check (and cash it) to bring the fund back to the desired level (most likely between $10.00 and $40.00). Be sure to transfer the transactions to your Petty Cash Journal and/or your Disbursements Journal.

COMMON ESTIMATED BUSINESS EXPENSES —

INITIAL EXPENSES	ESTIMATED COST
Opening Business Checking Account	$ 500.00
Telephone Installation	$ 200.00
Approximately $100 deposit per line, $80 connection fee, plus wiring charges.	
Equipment	$?
First & Last Months Rent & Security Deposit	$1000.00
Business Cards	$ 100.00
Stationery & Envelopes	$ 125.00
Brochure	$ 250.00
Logo	$ 250.00
Advertising Package (OPTIONAL)	$1000.00
ads in local papers, magazines, radio—	
Decorations	$ 150.00
Office Supplies	$ 300.00
Furniture, Music System, Tapes, Clothes	$?

ANNUAL EXPENSES:	
Property Insurance	$ 175.00
Auto Insurance	$ 500.00
Business License	$ 100.00
Liability Insurance	$ 250.00
Professional Society Membership	$ 300.00
Legal & Accounting Fees	$ 400.00

MONTHLY EXPENSES:	
Rent	$ 350.00
Utilities	$ 50.00
Telephone	$ 50.00
Bank fees	$ 5.00
Supplies	$ 50.00
Networking Club Dues	$ 40.00
Education (seminars, books, journals...)	$ 40.00
Medical Insurance	$ 150.00
Auto (payme--- gas, repairs...)	$ 300.00
Pr---	$ 100.00
	$ 15.00
	$ 30.00
ce (also cleaning service)	$ 70.00
	$ 20.00
mately $6.00 per line)	$ 12.00
s	$?
	$?

SAMPLE MONTHLY INCOME LEDGER SHEET

Month _____ 19 _____ Page _____

Date	Client Name	$ Amount Paid	Check #	Barter	Promo	Client Type	Location	Company	Client Type
4/2	Susan Smith	25.00	312			O	Outcall-Office	ABC Corp.	
4/2	Brad Jones	20.00	1947			O	Outcall-Office	ABC Corp.	
4/2	Amy Allen	25.00	417			N	Office	Humane Society	
4/3	Bill Peters	0.00	Cash			O	Outcall-Home	Attorney	Prepaid Services
4/3	Chris Evans	35.00	Cash			N	Office	Evans & Assoc.	
4/7	Jill Andrews	0.00				N	Office	T & J Accounting	Gift Certificate
4/7	Gregg Adams	40.00	Cash			O	Office	Artist	
4/7	John Carson				X	N	Office	Stars R Us	Knows many people
4/8	Don Connelly	30.00	653			N	Office	Thornton Co.	
4/8	Sue/Joe Roberts	75.00	712			O	Outcall-Home	XYZ Corp.	
4/12	Bill Peters	0.00				O	Outcall-Home		
4/12	Mary Saunders	30.00	211			N	Office	N/A	
4/14	Chris Evans	35.00	506			O	Office		
4/14	Paula Anderson	30.00	614			O	Office	School District	
4/14	Alice Crawford	35.00	430			O	Office	TMJ Corp.	
4/19	Steve Petry	25.00	Cash			O	Office	Allied Assoc.	
4/19	Jay Park			($30.00)		N	Office	Carpenter	Trade for bookcases
4/22	Bill Peters	0.00				O	Outcall-Home		
4/23	Janet Woods	30.00	347			N	Office	Model	Refered by Carson
4/26	Cheryl Jackson	125.00	940			O	Office	Burns & Assoc.	Series of 5
4/26	Susan Smith	20.00	330			O	Outcall-Office		
4/26	Brad Jones	25.00	1962			O	Outcall-Office		
4/26	Jay Parker			($30.00)		O	Office		
4/27	Chris Evans	35.00	Cash			O	Office		
4/27	Sue/Joe Roberts	75.00	746			O	Outcall-Home		
4/29	Miriam Fields	35.00	810			N	Office	Data Tech	
4/29	Paul Davis	40.00	Cash			O	Office		Very long session
4/29	Jeff Green	30.00	123			N	Office	M & M Inc.	

Total Income $ 850.00   Total Barter $ 60.00   Total # of Sessions 31   New Clients: 10   Ongoing: 14

SAMPLE MONTHLY DISBURSEMENTS LEDGER SHEET

Month _____ 19 ____ Page ____

Date	Description	Check #	Check Amount	Rent Utilities	Maintenance Telephone	Supplies Postage	Promotion Advertising	Travel Auto	Furniture Equipment	License Dues	Education Insurance	Books Inventory	Bank Fees Entertainment	Misc. Draw
4/2	ABA	140	250.00							D 250.00				
4/2	Jones Cleaning	141	27.00		M 27.00									
4/2	Paul's Auto.	142	17.30					A 17.30						
4/2	Sunset Bldg.	143	225.00	R 225.00										
4/3	Gas ToFo	Cash	9.00					A 9.00						
4/4	RJ Office Prod.	144	6.21			S 6.21								
4/4	Pace Printers	145	29.50				P 29.50							
4/4	The Last Cafe	Cash	12.70										E 12.70	
4/10	The Gardens	146	18.40										E 18.40	
4/12	Phone Co.	147	45.90		T 45.90									
4/12	Success First	148	20.00							D 20.00				
4/17	Career Seminars	149	50.00								E 50.00			
4/17	"Your Name"	150	400.00											D 400.00
4/18	Discount Supp.	Cash	8.14			S 8.14								
4/19	National Bank		4.20										B 4.20	
4/20	Ace Insurance	151	200.00								I 200.00			
4/21	US Postal Ser.	152	25.00			P 25.00								
4/25	Earth Times	153	60.00				A 60.00							
4/25	AAA Utilities	154	50.00	U 50.00										
4/26	Discount Supp.	155	10.00			S 10.00								
TOTAL			1468.35	275.00	72.90	49.35	89.50	26.30		270.00	250.00		35.30	400.00

*Please note that not all expenses are 100% deductible. Please consult current tax laws.

SAMPLE CASH FLOW PROJECTIONS SHEET —

	MAY	JUNE	JULY	TOTALS
BEGINNING CASH	1850	2200	945	1850
PLUS MONTHLY INCOME FROM:				
Fees	2100	1200	2300	5600
Sales	0	0	0	0
Loans	0	0	0	0
Other	0	0	0	0
TOTAL CASH AND INCOME	**3950**	**3400**	**3245**	**7450**
EXPENSES:				
Rent	350	350	350	1050
Utilities	40	55	55	150
Telephone	50	50	50	150
Bank Fees	5	5	5	15
Supplies	75	10	65	150
Stationery & Business Cards	0	100	0	100
Insurance	0	650	0	650
Dues	75	0	325	400
Education	20	200	0	220
Auto	300	300	300	900
Advertising & Promotion	100	50	50	200
Postage	10	0	35	45
Entertainment	40	30	20	90
Repair & Maintenance	80	50	80	210
Travel	0	70	0	70
Business Loan Payments	0	0	0	0
Licenses & Permits	0	0	75	75
Salary/Draw	500	500	500	1500
Staff Salaries	0	0	0	0
Taxes	0	0	600	600
Professional Fees	35	35	30	100
Decorations	20	0	0	20
Furniture & Fixtures	50	0	0	50
Equipment	0	0	425	425
Inventory	0	0	0	0
Other Expenses	0	0	0	0
TOTAL EXPENSES	**1750**	**2455**	**2965**	**7170**
ENDING CASH (+ or -)	**2200**	**945**	**280**	**280**

• FEDERAL TAXES •

The topic of taxation has become enshrouded in an aura of mystique. Many people believe that cutting taxes means hiring high-priced experts to find "loopholes" in the law (a technique only for rich people). The law is the same for everyone, and tax-cutting strategies are available to all.

No one is required to pay more tax than the law demands. Some of the more common tax-cutting strategies are:

SPLITTING INCOME among several family members (age 14 and older) or legal entities in order to get more of the income taxed at lower brackets.

SHIFTING INCOME from one year to another in order to have it fall where it will be taxed at lower rates.

SHIFTING DEDUCTIONS from one year to another in order to place them where the tax benefit will be greater.

DEFERRING TAX LIABILITY through certain investments and pension plan contributions.

STRUCTURING YOUR BUSINESS to obtain a tax deduction for some expenses paid for things you enjoy (e.g., travel).

INVESTING YOUR MONEY to produce income that is exempt from either (or both) federal and state income tax.

I highly recommend you consult with an accountant regarding tax matters. Unless your financial affairs are extremely simple, chances are that you will overlook deductions and credits to which you are entitled. A professional tax preparer knows what to look for and what's available to reduce your tax bill. While it's important for you to be familiar with the general workings of tax planning and the tax law — leave the technical details to your accountant.

Think of this in terms of your own practice. The general public might be able to handle their well-being on their own, but they come to you because you are supposed to have a higher degree of knowledge, experience, objectivity and techniques than they possess. If you expect people to use your services, it's imperative that you also utilize appropriate allied professionals.

IRS REQUIRED FORMS —

If you are self-employed and earn more than $400.00 you must file:

- **Schedule SE**: Social Security Self-Employment Tax Form

- **Schedule C**: Sole Proprietorship Business or Profession Profit or Loss Form

- **Form 1040**: U.S. Individual Income Tax Return

- **Form 1040 ES**: Estimated Tax For Individuals (if you expect to owe taxes)

- **Form 1099**: Any employer who pays more than $600.00 to a self-employed person must report that payment to the IRS and to the sub-contractor

- **Form 1065 K-1**: Partnership Information Return (for a business owned by two or more individuals)

Business Deductions —

Business owners are entitled to numerous deductions. (Please refer to the list of Common Business Expenses on page 18). Most of these expenses (except for those such as personal draw) are recognized as full deductions on Schedule C although some of these allowances have strict guidelines and ceilings, particularly the business use of the home, travel and entertainment, transportation and equipment purchases. If you want additional information, call the IRS at (800) 829-3676 to request the publications that decipher their requirements.

Business Use of Home

You can deduct expenses that are related to using a part of the home regularly and exclusively as either a principal place of business or as a place to meet clients. The percentage of business use of a home is determined by dividing the square feet of the business space by the total square feet of the home. If the space was used for less than a full year, you must prorate expenses for the number of months used for the business.

100% of the cost of decorating, furnishing, repairs and maintenance of the business-use space is deductible or depreciable. The business percentage of permanent improvements that benefit the entire home (e.g., new roof or temperature control unit) are depreciable.

Deductions for the business use of a home may not be used to create a business loss or increase a net loss from a business. Deductions in excess of that limit may be carried forward to later years (subject to the income limits in those years). Also, if you deduct office space in your home, you may be subject to a capital gains tax upon the sale of your house. Certain time parameters are involved, so consult with an accountant and plan appropriate strategies.

Travel and Entertainment

It is essential to keep accurate records to substantiate all travel and entertainment expenses. In regards to gifts for clients, you are allowed to declare $25.00 per client per year. The deduction for business-related meals and entertainment is limited to a maximum of 80%. If you have to travel any distance for business, the actual transportation and lodging costs are usually 100% deductible (although an unusual number of trips to exotic locales might be grounds for an audit).

The records you keep must be supported by adequate evidence such as receipts, canceled checks and credit card statements. Keep a journal that denotes (for each expense) a description of the expense; the amount spent; date, time and place; business purpose; names and business relationship of person(s) entertained or gifted; and any other pertinent information.

Transportation

The customary and necessary expenses incurred on operating and maintaining a vehicle for business purposes is deductible according to the actual percentage of business use.

The two methods for computing allowable expenses are the actual expenses (at the business-use percentage) or the total business mileage (using the IRS determined allowance). You must use actual costs if you use more than one vehicle in your business.

The best evidence to support a transportation deduction is a logbook that shows the date, business purpose, destination and mileage of all business travel (see Appendix A).

FILING YOUR RETURNS —

January 15: Fourth installment of previous year's estimated tax.

January 31: Businesses must furnish 1099s to sub-contractors.

Employers must furnish W-2 statements to employees.

Employers must file previous year's unemployment tax returns and pay any tax due.

February 28: Businesses must file information returns (e.g., 1099) with IRS.

Employers must send W-2 copies to Social Security Administration.

March 15: Previous calendar year corporation income tax returns due.

April 15: Deadline for individual tax returns. In addition to Form 1040 (and appropriate accompanying schedules) include the requisite business forms such as: 1065 K-1, Schedules SE and C.
First installment of current year's estimated tax.

July 15: Second installment of current year's estimated tax.

October 15: Third installment of current year's estimated tax.

ESTIMATED TAX PAYMENTS —

Generally, you must pay estimated tax if you expect to owe (after subtracting your withholding and credits) at least $500.00 in tax for this current year, and you expect your withholding and credits to be less than:

1. 90% of the tax to be shown on current year tax return — OR —

2. 100% of the tax shown on the previous year tax return (given the return covered all twelve months).

The exception to this is if your previous year tax return showed a refund or the tax balance due was less than $500.00. The caveat being that if your income is at a level where you will need to pay taxes (even if you can avoid making prepayments to the IRS this year), set up a "savings" account for that money.

RECORD KEEPING —

IRS regulations require taxpayers to keep records and receipts for as long as they may be applicable to the enforcement of tax law. For income and expenses, this is usually the later of three years from the date the return was filed or two years after the tax was paid.

Records related to the basis (cost) of property should be kept indefinitely (e.g., papers related to the purchase of real estate and equipment). Copies of tax returns should be kept for at least ten years.

If you are documenting your work and keeping accurate accounts, then tax preparation becomes a natural extension of your bookkeeping activities. The initial establishment of your bookkeeping system will take some thought and time. After that, if you update your books on a regular basis, you will find that it doesn't take much effort or time to maintain accurate records.

• INSURANCE BILLING •

Accepting insurance can be an incredible asset to your business. Often times it can be the determining factor in whether or not a potential client actually chooses you to be their health care provider. Unfortunately, if you are not recognized by the insurance companies as a "primary" health giver, this process can be cumbersome. Many insurance companies are more inclined to honor insurance claims if you work for/with an MD or a DO (and sometimes a NC or DC) and the doctor does the billing. The three types of major insurance claims are: third party (general medical health), worker's compensation and personal injury.

General medical health policies vary greatly not only between carriers but even within each company. You may have conflicting experiences from the same carrier due to a difference in the terms of the policies. For example, you may have gotten prompt repayment one time and then the next time been refused payment for the same exact service — the distinction being that it was with two different clients and thus two separate policies. So, even if you are considered a primary health provider, it's recommended that you also verify each policy as to its specific requirements and allowances. You can't always predict whether the company will authorize payments, the total amount they will cover or the number of sessions they will allow....

Worker's compensation supplies a significant amount of the money that goes toward health care. In order to receive direct payment under worker's compensation, you need to have a health care provider's number. If you are a primary care giver, you can use your identification number in most states. Some states require a separate number. If you are not the primary care giver, you usually can still receive a code number — but you also must get a prescriptive referral from the primary care giver for each case. You need to consult with the proper agency to get accurate information for obtaining your number and learning the required procedures for filling out the paperwork. There isn't a national bureau, so you have to contact the agency for your specific state. To find the agency, look under the state government section in the phone book for a category titled either State Compensation Fund, Industrial Worker's Insurance or Worker's Compensation Board. If you still are unable to locate the appropriate agency, call the general information number.

Personal injury claims are handled differently than most other types of insurance cases. Customarily, you submit the bill directly to the claims adjuster or the attorney. In most instances, they will cover everything. Again, if you are not the attending physician, you will need a prescription from one. One of the drawbacks to working with personal injury clients is that you usually don't receive payment for your services until the case is resolved (which sometimes takes years).

It is advisable to check with the insurance carrier for each client. You may need to call the local representative to get the name and number of the person with whom to talk at the main office. It can be very helpful in receiving payment if you get pre-approval for services. ALWAYS note the name of the person you are talking with and (if possible) get a code for approved service. You can spend a lot of time in verifying policies and filling out paperwork. That is why many practitioners don't accept insurance claims — they require the client to pay them directly for the services, and then the client must submit a voucher to his/her own insurance company (or attorney) for reimbursement. If you decide to incorporate insurance billing into your practice, please purchase a comprehensive book on insurance reimbursement that will completely guide you through the correct procedures. You must balance the positive and negative aspects involved in accepting health insurance, realizing that as your business grows, you may change your mind.

• POLICIES AND PROCEDURES •

With respect to business operations, it's almost an imperative to have written policies and procedures (particularly if you are in a group practice). This is pertinent even if you work for someone else. Discuss the desired policies and procedures with your employer/employees. You may find that you can add or even alter them. Policies are generally divided into two branches — internal company policies and client interaction policies. Policies are built on your philosophy regarding your practice whereas procedures are specific steps based on how you want to run the day-to-day details of the business. A policies and procedures manual sets the tone for your business and helps you avoid potential conflicts.

A procedure manual defines the methods you have chosen to operate your business. In creating your procedure manual, begin by describing how you want to commence each working day. Then delineate the important daily activities. Include the way you want clients to be greeted, the handling of paperwork and client files (particularly crucial if you are billing insurance), the care and operation of equipment, how to write up sales, safety procedures and what to do in case of an emergency, bookkeeping, the desired manner for carrying out routine business activities and the procedures for closing the business at the end of the day.

Internal company policies are necessary if you have employees. In designing a policy manual, begin with a statement of your company's purpose, priorities and goals. Then describe your qualifications, requirements and expectations of your staff. Be certain to explain exactly how you want these policies manifested. Include general personality requirements, educational standards, chain of command, work hours and schedule, salary, raises, overtime, pay day, leaves of absence, tardiness, sick leave, bonuses, benefits package, reviews and evaluations, personnel records, grievances procedures, use of phone, dress and hygiene, smoking, medication, parking, employee purchasing procedures and discounts (of services or product), actions requiring discipline and specific consequences, disciplinary procedures, grounds for termination and (most importantly) customer relations.

Client interaction policies are vital to your peace of mind. Some things to consider in developing your policies are: How do you want to deal with people who are late or just don't show up? What will you do if someone doesn't pay you or his/her check bounces? (Please note that in most states you can go to the bank from where the check is drawn and obtain preferential status in getting the check cashed as soon as funds are deposited into the account). What will you do if a client makes sexual advances or behaves inappropriately in general? What degree of honesty and self-disclosure will you require of your clients? How available will you be to your clients (e.g., giving them support or answering questions on the telephone, after hours), under what conditions and for what length of time? Under what circumstances will you offer a reduced rate? How much notice will you require for cancellations?

In most areas, there are no "right" ways to set up client interaction policies. You must do what feels right for you. Be certain to only have policies that you are willing to enforce. Although it's best to establish your policies before you start your practice, you can create and refine them at any time. You may want to list your policies on your client intake forms, post them or verbally state them to all of your clients. By having clear policies, neither you nor your clients will feel awkward — you know what to expect from each other. It is also important to be flexible, but you can decide ahead of time what circumstances are acceptable and include those in your policies.

Describe your philosophy towards your profession in general:

_____

_____

_____

_____

_____

_____

_____

_____

Describe your philosophy towards your business in particular:

_____

_____

_____

_____

_____

_____

_____

_____

_____

Describe how you want to run your business:

_____

_____

_____

_____

_____

_____

_____

_____

_____

Sketch your procedure manual:

_____

_____

_____

_____

_____

_____

_____

_____

_____

_____

List your policies for staff:

_____

_____

_____

_____

_____

_____

_____

List your policies for clients:

_____

_____

_____

_____

_____

_____

_____

_____

CHAPTER FIVE

MARKETING

MARKETING

• INTRODUCTION •

The word "marketing" conjures up an amazing array of thoughts and feelings ranging from studied disinterest to confusion to hand-wringing dismay. Many people automatically associate marketing with hard-sell tactics. Force isn't a requirement in sales.

Marketing is simply all the business activities done on a daily basis to attract potential clients in order for them to utilize/buy your services. These activities include promotion, sales and advertising. It is about enabling your clientele to value you and your services.

Marketing a service is very different than marketing a product. For example, retailers tend to use mass marketing techniques such as broad-based advertising campaigns, direct mailings, telemarketing and in-store promotions. Service businesses usually target a very well-defined market and use a more personal approach. The major portion of marketing a service business is educational in nature.

Marketing plans address the following questions: Where are you now? Where do you want to be? How do you get there? There's a saying that goes, "If you don't know where you are going, what matters the path?" This is so true in any type of planning — especially with marketing. All too often healing arts practitioners leave their marketing to chance. They wait for people to find them, an attitude that generally isn't productive. (It is okay if you have an alternate source of income.) But, then again, think about why you got into this field in the first place. What good does it do to want to enhance people's well-being if the people don't know who you are? You don't have to employ the same techniques that "big business" does. You can incorporate other methods such as public speaking, visualizations and affirmations. The critical point here is that you do create some type of marketing plan with the focus primarily being on promotion.

Promotion is about getting yourself known, about building a professional reputation. The ultimate aim of promotion is to develop a thriving practice, and that means having a strong and continually growing clientele base.

A strange paradox of competition versus abundance exists in this career field. On one hand, there truly are enough potential clients in the world for everyone, and yet on the other hand, not many healing arts practitioners have as many clients as they want. Part of the dilemma stems from the fact that the people are "potential" clients. You have to make them aware of you and the benefits of your services. It is not as though there are limitless numbers of people anxiously waiting for you to let them know you exist. You must create the need. Unfortunately, many people still don't recognize the value of the healing arts. Obviously, some of us know better.

What you are really competing with is a lack of knowledge on part of the general public, thus the necessity of including some type of direct education (e.g., writing articles, giving demonstrations, public speaking, and compiling information packets) in your marketing plan.

Even though competition has been historically associated with struggle and rivalry it doesn't have to be that way any more. Think of competition as a way of distinguishing yourself from the other healing arts practitioners. One of the most exciting facets of this industry is that people usually aren't attempting to prove that they're "better" than another practitioner — but that they're different. That is why promotion is vital to your career. You have to sell people on your services and then on you! It is not wise to assume that you are going to attract the people who "know better", take care of themselves and use alternative health services. Such people probably already have a regular practitioner. So, you are going to have to create a new market and possibly share some of the existing market.

Actually, your marketing ventures will be significantly more successful and enjoyable if you participate with other practitioners in joint promotional activities. Develop a working relationship with at least two other practitioners: one person who does similar work as you but is targeting a different market, and another practitioner in an allied field that shares your target market.

Combine some of your marketing tasks; not only will you save money and time, but the synergistic energy can be incredible! The creative process works best with more than one person. Also, by pooling your resources, you may find yourself able to afford other promotional projects such as joint mailings, shared booth space at conventions and co-operative advertising. Another benefit of having a marketing colleague is that public presentations and demonstrations are much less intimidating and have greater impact when done by two people. Some of the most dreaded aspects of marketing become less of a chore (and often are a lot of fun) when you don't have to do them alone.

Remember that in this field, marketing centers around educating the public. Keep this in mind when developing your strategies. Don't take it for granted that people "know" what you do because you have a certain title. Define what you do. Explain the benefits of what you offer and clarify your Differential Advantage. Every practitioner is unique, and brings her/his experience and personality into play along with whatever techniques are employed. The power of your marketing increases with the level in which you integrate YOU into those marketing strategies.

Successful marketing is based on having a clear vision for your business, defining your target markets, clarifying your differential advantage, determining your position statement, and designing a marketing plan that utilizes creative and effective strategies which reflect your values. This chapter takes you through the whole process in order to support you in building and maintaining a growing, thriving clientele base.

• OUTLINE •

The chart below illustrates the major components of a marketing plan. The subsequent pages contain exercises as well as technical information to assist you in preparing for the final creation of your marketing plan (refer to Chapter Six).

I • OVERVIEW (PURPOSE, PRIORITIES AND GOALS)
Statement of why you are in this business

Results you intend to create

Summary of how you will accomplish your goals

II • TARGET MARKET ANALYSIS
Demographics

Psychographics

III • POSITION STATEMENT
Image

Differential Advantage

IV • MARKETING ASSESSMENT
Analysis of previous promotional activities

Recommended changes for future plans

Overview of competition's marketing

V • STRATEGIC ACTION PLANS
Promotion

Advertising

Time tables

• OVERVIEW •

To develop effective marketing strategies you must first clarify your purpose, priorities and goals and then determine how you will implement your marketing plan. The answers to the following questions will assist you in making the appropriate choices for your promotion and advertising campaigns.

Why you are in this business?

_____
_____
_____
_____

What is your purpose for marketing?

_____
_____
_____
_____

What are your priorities for marketing?

_____
_____
_____
_____

What are your major goals for marketing?

_____
_____
_____
_____

What are your strategies for accomplishing these results?

_____
_____
_____
_____

• TARGET MARKET ANALYSIS •

Before you can create a successful marketing campaign, it's necessary to determine your target market (toward whom to direct your energies). The whole concept of target marketing can seem very scary at first. On the surface, targeting appears to be limiting the scope of the pool of potential clients. Many people fear that by defining a market, they will lose business. They are concerned that they will choose the wrong market. The other major concern is that the other practitioners will take just anybody and therefore some of their business.

You must keep in mind that the purpose of defining your target market is to make your life easier and increase the productivity of your promotional endeavors. Many opportunities exist in this world and it's impossible to pursue them all or be everything to everyone. You need to know where to focus your energy and money when it comes to promotion and advertising.

Target Marketing and Positioning go hand-in-hand. It is difficult to explain one without the other. As a matter of fact, if you have more than one target market (which is usually wise), and they are vastly different, you may need a separate position statement for each of those target markets. In order to make this subject more comprehensible, I recommend that you scan both topics (this and the following section), and then study each one in depth.

Choosing several markets is one of the best ways to avoid the potential disaster of selecting an unsuitable market. The benefits of not being restricted to only one type of clientele are numerous. Your skills become well-rounded by experiencing a variety of people with their own unique issues and all of your eggs won't be in one basket in case you indeed chose an inappropriate market.

The two most common means of market analysis are demographics and psychographics, which describe a person in terms of objective data and personality attributes.

DEMOGRAPHICS ARE STATISTICS SUCH AS:

- Age
- Gender
- Income Level
- Geographic Location
- Occupation
- Education Level

PSYCHOGRAPHICS ARE LIFESTYLE FACTORS INCLUDING:

- Special Interest Activities
- Philosophical Beliefs
- Social Factors
- Cultural Involvements

The more you know about your potential clients, the easier it is to develop an appropriate position statement and design an effective marketing campaign. The actual number of target markets you have depends mainly upon the size of your practice and the scope of your knowledge.

TARGET MARKET ANALYSIS EXAMPLES —

A MASSAGE THERAPIST has an office in a medical plaza. He specializes in sports massage and deep tissue therapy.

HIS CLIENTELE HAVE THESE CHARACTERISTICS:

- Thirty percent were referred by other health care providers in the building.

- Forty percent were referred by friends and other clients.

- Thirty percent responded to an advertisement.

- The majority had been experiencing pain.

- The average age range is between 21 and 47 years old.

- Half of them are currently under the care of another allied practitioner.

- Seventy percent read the local weekly entertainment publication.

- Forty percent had never had a professional massage.

- Sixty percent attend at least one concert each year.

- The majority are genuinely interested in self-improvement.

- Fifteen percent are competition athletes.

- Their combined family income is greater than $35,000.00.

These statistics provide the basis for determining his target markets. This massage therapist could easily develop three distinct markets: clients that are referred from other health care providers, a general practice and competitive athletes.

He would need to develop at least two position statements. The position statement that is geared to the client itself could be the same for the referral and general market (although it is wise to consider the referring practitioners as a separate market). The athletic market needs its own position statement.

He can take this information and develop a target market profile. Let's use the athletic market as an example:

> *"My typical competitive athlete client is a 28 year old male. He has been referred to me by a physician or by someone at the gym. His reasons for utilizing my services center around pain management and improving his overall athletic performance. He schedules sessions weekly for two months, then tapers to twice per month. He competes in at least one major sporting event each month and has had at least one serious injury in the past three years. He holds either a supervisory or technical position at work and earns at least $25,000.00 per year. He likes to attend concerts and casual community functions. He scans through the local weekly entertainment magazine and reads the fitness publications from cover to cover."*

Possible avenues of approaching this competitive athlete market include: doing promotions at local health clubs; getting interviewed by, placing an advertisement in, and/or writing an article for the local weekly entertainment magazine and any fitness publications; developing associations with those people involved in athletics (e.g., the athletes themselves, sports physicians and trainers); and volunteering his massage services at sporting events.

A **PSYCHOTHERAPIST** has an office in a downtown professional building. In addition to individual counseling services, she also has a "rejuvenation room" that can be rented in twenty minute increments. This room is furnished with a massage chair, self-hypnosis audio tapes and other relaxation equipment (such as a biofeedback machine). She has two different markets. First she has the clients that see her for personal development. Then she has another group of people that come in for quick stress reduction.

A PROFILE OF HER COUNSELING CLIENTS IS THAT:

- Seventy percent are women.

- The average age range is between 29 and 46 years old.

- They have a college degree (or equivalent).

- They value their personal growth.

- The majority are in management level positions or are business owners.

- Most of them are involved in a Twelve Step Program.

- Their combined family income is greater than $40,000.00.

THE CLIENTS THAT USE THE REJUVENATION ROOM HAVE THESE CHARACTERISTICS:

- Ninety percent of them work in the same building.

- The gender ratio is approximately equal.

- These people have stressful jobs.

- The average age range is between 24 and 58 years old.

- The majority hold staff level positions.

- Sixty percent subscribe to three or more business publications.

- Many are single with an income of less than $30,000.00.

- Fifty percent attend at least two cultural events per year.

In this example, the psychotherapist actually has two separate businesses with at least two markets. Some cross-over may occur between the businesses, so it would be wise for her to develop complementary position statements.

Her profile for the rejuvenation room clients might look like this:

> *"My typical client is a single 32 year old that earns less than $30,000.00 per year. This person works under high pressure conditions. S/he has held a job in this building for more than two years. This person schedules a twenty minute time slot in the rejuvenation room once per week and at least once per month books the room for an hour. Whenever the client is not busy working, s/he enjoys attending cultural events and reading professional publications."*

Possible avenues for approaching this rejuvenation room target market include: posting promotional material on the bulletin boards in the common areas; putting fliers/coupons on the cars in the parking lot; giving free (or nominal cost) lunch-time seminars on such topics as stress reduction, healthy lifestyles and peak performance; hosting regular introductory seminars and demonstrations; submitting employee well-being proposals to the owners and managers of the other companies; and holding monthly open houses.

YOUR TARGET MARKET PROFILE —

In order to clarify your target market(s) you need to delineate the demographic and psychographic factors and then identify the characteristics your clients have in common.

Describe your current clients and those who are most likely your future clients:

What is the age range and average age of your clients? _____

What is the percentage of males? _____ %   females? _____ %

What is the average educational level of your clients? _____

Where do your clients live? _____

What are the occupations of your clients? _____

_____

_____

Where do your clients work? _____

_____

_____

What is average annual income level of your clients? $ _____

Of which special interest groups are your clients members? _____

_____

_____

_____

What attitudes and beliefs about health care do your clients hold? _____

_____

_____

_____

What is the primary reason your clients use your services? _____

_____

_____

What are some of the other reasons your clients use your services? _____

_____

_____

_____

What is the average number of sessions per client? _____

How many clients come in weekly? _____   bimonthly? _____   monthly? _____

more than once per week? _____   occasionally? _____

DEFINING YOUR TARGET MARKET(S) —

Write a descriptive statement for each of your target markets (Refer to your "Target Market Profile"). Include a brief overview of the services you are providing to that group and a detailed analysis of the characteristics of the specific clientele.

TARGET MARKET 1:

_____

_____

_____

_____

_____

_____

_____

TARGET MARKET 2:

_____

_____

_____

_____

_____

_____

_____

TARGET MARKET 3:

_____

_____

_____

_____

_____

_____

_____

• POSITION STATEMENT •

Positioning is the key principle of marketing. You must determine exactly what niche you intend to fill. Most businesses have weak or nonexistent positions in the minds of the consumers. Prospective clients need an easy way to differentiate you from your competition. Your position statement provides that information.

Three examples of successful positioning statements are those from Avis, Vicks and Seven-Up. Everyone knows that Seven-Up's marketing position is: "Seven-Up, The Uncola." At the time that Seven-Up was developing its marketing campaign, a soda usually meant Coca-Cola or Pepsi. To counteract that assumption, they promoted their product as something totally "un"like the other popular soft drinks.

When the Vicks Company was preparing to promote its new formula, the market was controlled by Contact and Dristan. Instead of attempting to take away some of their share of the market, Vicks created a new one. Thus, the introduction of NyQuil, "The Nightime, Sniffling, Sneezing, Coughing, Aching, Stuffy Head, Fever, So You Can Rest Medicine".

Avis took an innovative (and highly effective) approach in their positioning. They had to overcome two problems: another company already had a strong hold on the number one position, (can you name it?) and most people find it extremely difficult to differentiate one car rental business from another. Their solution was the slogan, "We're Avis. We're Number Two. We Try Harder." This position statement distinguishes Avis from the other companies and makes a compelling promise to its potential customers.

Image plays a major role in your positioning. Decide the type of impression you want to give (refer to Chapter Three). Write a paragraph that summarizes the image you wish to portray:

_____

_____

_____

_____

_____

_____

_____

_____

_____

_____

_____

_____

Now you need to assess whether or not your facilities, actions and attire align with this image. If they don't, you need to make some choices before you continue developing your position statement. You have to either redefine your image or alter the elements that are not in sync with your desired image.

THE DIFFERENTIAL ADVANTAGE —

Defining your Differential Advantage is the next step in creating your position statement. By answering the following questions, you clarify your Differential Advantage. Do this exercise for each of your target markets:

What does your business do?

_____

_____

_____

_____

What needs does your business meet?

_____

_____

_____

_____

What problems does your business solve?

_____

_____

_____

_____

How will your clients benefit psychologically?

_____

_____

_____

_____

How does your business differ from the competition?

_____

_____

_____

_____

Position Statement Examples —

The following position statements illustrate the range of possible differential advantages from types of services, to philosophy, to specific clientele and to location. Position statements are similar to slogans, though not always so catchy.

Services

Some position statements are based solely upon the service(s) provided. This approach is usually taken when a practitioner has specialized knowledge, a unique service, a particularly clever slogan or state-of-the-art equipment.

"On Pins And Needles? Try Acupuncture For Relief"

"We Use The Latest Advances In Dental Technology"

"The Only Certified Practitioner In The Midwest"

"Trained By The Founder Of <insert well-known name here>"

"We Use An Array Of Modalities"

Philosophy

Most healing arts practitioners have strong beliefs about the nature of well-being and their particular approach to health care. Quite often, this is the major quality that distinguishes one practitioner from another.

"We Treat You As A Whole Person"

"Your Well-Being Is Our Purpose"

"The Beginning Of A Healthy Lifestyle"

"Helping People To Get In Touch With Their Selves"

"The First Thing We Do Is Listen"

"Your Kids Have A Voice With Us"

"Supporting You In Creating Success, While Keeping Balance"

"The Gentle Approach To Deep Tissue Therapy"

"Our Touch Helps You Get In Touch With Yourself"

"We Use Holistic Methods Whenever Possible"

"Combining Ancient Healing Wisdom With State-Of-The-Art Technology"

Specialization

Some position statements are based on appealing to a target market. For example, you may prefer to only work with one gender or a specific age group. Maybe your focus is treating a specific condition or part of the body.

"Seniors Are Our Specialty"

"Woman to Woman"

"Making Your Pregnancy More Comfortable"

"Giving Athletes That Competitive Edge"

"My Hands For Your Feet"

"Helping You Overcome Your Phobias"

"We Work Exclusively With ACoAs"

"The Specialists In Neck And Head Injuries"

OFFICE LOCATION

Your location can play a significant role in your business. It may be your strongest differential advantage. For example, if your office is located in a sizable professional building, your appeal is accessibility — people can have appointments on their breaks, they don't have to drive, etc. If you do out-calls, capitalize on convenience — they don't have to go anywhere or do anything... Perhaps your office is more of a retreat. If that's the case, then expound upon the relaxing "get-away" qualities.

> *"The Healthy Coffee Break Alternative"*
>
> *"Have Table, Will Travel"*
>
> *"Providing All Your Health Care Needs In One Location"*
>
> *"A Haven From The Hectic Workplace"*
>
> *"Too Stressed To Leave Home? We Make House Calls"*
>
> *"Only Twenty Minutes From Downtown, Yet A World Apart"*
>
> *"A Health Oasis In The Desert"*

YOUR POSITION STATEMENT —

Review your responses to the differential advantage questions and highlight the most important facets. Then combine those with your image statement to formulate your position statement:

_____

_____

_____

_____

_____

_____

_____

_____

_____

_____

_____

_____

_____

_____

Now evaluate your position statement in terms of the following criteria: Does it appeal to your target market? Do you need to change your target market? Is it a true benefit? Does it differentiate you from your competition? Is it unique?

• ASSESSMENT •

YOU —

The next phase in developing your marketing plan is the assessment of your previous promotional endeavors and those of your competition. Listed below are some common methods for promotion and advertising. In the left-hand column, note how often you've already used these methods to market yourself and/or your services. Use "O" for often, "S" for sporadically and "N" for not at all. Then in the right-hand column, rate the effectiveness for each format. Use a scale of 1-10, with 1 being totally ineffective, 5 being moderately effective (a reasonable return for your time and money) and 10 being outstanding.

USAGE	METHODS	RATING
_____	Business cards	_____
_____	Brochures	_____
_____	Direct mail	_____
_____	Signs	_____
_____	Word-of-mouth	_____
_____	Newspaper	_____
_____	Television	_____
_____	Radio	_____
_____	Direct calling	_____
_____	Expos & health fairs	_____
_____	Special promo & displays	_____
_____	Networking	_____
_____	Writing articles	_____
_____	Professional journals	_____
_____	Introductory seminars	_____
_____	Demonstrations	_____
_____	Phone book	_____
_____	Press releases	_____
_____	Public speaking	_____
_____	Direct referrals	_____

If you offer more than one service, have you promoted each one?

❑ yes   ❑ no

If no, why? _____

_____

_____

_____

_____

Have you been satisfied with the quality of your marketing efforts?

❑ yes   ❑ no

If no, why? _____

_____

_____

_____

_____

What have been the results of your promotional activities so far?

_____

_____

_____

_____

_____

_____

_____

_____

What changes would you like to see happen?

_____

_____

_____

_____

_____

_____

_____

_____

YOUR COMPETITORS —

Now that you have assessed your previous marketing efforts, evaluate the competition (see Chapter Six). Unfortunately, this most likely won't be a straightforward task. You need to do some footwork. It can be easy to ignore this phase, since many practitioners aren't willing to challenge their precepts about competition. Yet the more you know about your competition, the easier it is for you to determine the best ways to promote your practice.

The first step is to identify just exactly who is your competition. Begin your research by studying the phone book. For example, you look through the phone book and discover that forty other practitioners are listed. Of those forty, perhaps half of them appear to provide similar services as yours. Find out more about them: Give them a call, request brochures and use their services. You may discover that only four or five of these people are in direct competition with you — that is, actually offer similar services to the same market at a comparable rate. The key being the **SAME** target market.

Meanwhile, take note of who is advertising in other local publications (you may want to get several months worth of editions). Notice whether or not your competitors are listed in any of those publications. Some good sources for brochures and fliers are bulletin boards at health food stores, offices of other practitioners and bookstores. Ascertain who is doing what and where they are doing it. These local publications and bulletin boards may be your primary source of information about your competitors since many healing arts practitioners don't advertise in the phone book.

Compile a profile on each of your major competitors. Include the following information:

- Name

- Location

- Length of time in business

- Description of services offered

- Manner in which services are provided

- Fee structure

- Clientele description

- Business strengths and limitations

- Differential advantage

- Market position

- Methods of promotion

The final step is to analyze the information you've collected. Look for patterns and trends. Then compare it to the assessment of your own business.

• STRATEGIC ACTION PLANS •

The final portion of the marketing plan is the actual design of your marketing campaign. Keep in mind all important dates e.g., holidays, clients' meaningful occasions and seasonal events (refer to the marketing plan outline in the business plan, Chapter Six).

Be aware that you may need separate promotional strategies for each target market.

For each strategy, ask yourself the following questions:

- Is the strategy realistic?

- Does this strategy fit into your budget?

- What are the ramifications of spending money on this strategy?

- Is this strategy unique?

- Is the market large enough to return a profit from this strategy?

- Does this strategy relate to your other strategies?

- Does this strategy accent your strengths and differences?

If your answer to any of these questions is no, it's highly recommended that you alter your strategy. If your answers are all yes, then it's time to put your marketing plan into action.

Implementing your marketing plan of action begins by setting up a schedule. Establish a timeline and specific deadlines for all the steps. Then, of course, you must stay on schedule. This is much easier to accomplish if you set realistic deadlines and integrate your goals into the timelines so they follow a logical order.

The next phase is to evaluate the results. If things are going as planned, review the rest of the plan to see if you can make any changes to further enhance the results. If you appear to be off target, identify the problems by asking yourself the following questions: Were the goals realistic? Was the timeline too ambitious? Did you need to rely upon too many outside factors? Did you expect more of a percentage increase than occurred? Were there any errors in your plan? Did you incorrectly add any of the numbers? Was any of your data inaccurate? Did you choose an inappropriate target market?

Once you've identified the obstacles, some possibilities for alleviating them are to change the basic goals, alter the timeline, correct the mistakes or possibly even change the overall strategy.

In summary, when developing your marketing campaign, you must: design your strategies (you may want to use a strategic planning form), determine your annual marketing budget, assess how well the plan is coordinated (see above questions) and then put the plan into action. It is important to evaluate the effectiveness of your campaign during each phase — and make any required changes.

The rest of this chapter covers the principles and specific promotional and advertising techniques for marketing your practice and retaining your clients.

• MARKETING TECHNIQUES OVERVIEW •

Now that you have clarified your purpose for being in this business, set your marketing purpose, priorities and goals, specified your target market(s), defined your differential advantage, composed your position statement, assessed your current marketing and evaluated your competition (whew!) — it's time to determine which methods to utilize in promoting your business.

Marketing embodies all of the activities and products involved in getting yourself known, which in turn brings you additional clients. Effective marketing can make the difference between a thriving business and a mediocre one.

Marketing techniques can be divided into three major categories: promotion, advertising and public relations. In essence, advertising is direct payment for publicity, promotion is indirect payment for publicity and public relations is free media exposure for your business.

Establishing credibility is essential to the long-term success of your practice and is the foundation of any successful marketing venture. Webster defines credible as "entitled to belief or trust; honorable; reliable." Your level of professionalism (Chapter Three) plays a major role in your credibility status. Your actions must complement your words. Don't make promises (either verbally or in printed materials) that you are unwilling to fulfill and don't make claims that you can't substantiate.

In designing your marketing strategies, be certain to include a good mix of techniques. Marketing your business takes a lot of time and creativity — particularly with a small practice. Don't always rely on previously used methods (even if they seemed to work), especially if you are approaching the same target group. People like and respond to variety. They don't want to see (or hear) the same thing over and over again. The other reason for altering your marketing modes is to reach potential clients that may not have been inspired by your earlier endeavors. You must use an assortment of approaches in an ongoing, consistent manner. Marketing never ends. It is an integral component of your business. Plan on investing at least fifteen percent of your time in marketing to maintain your practice and more to expand it. If you are just starting out, you may need to increase it to more than fifty percent.

The methods available for marketing your practice are unlimited (unless your specific profession has distinct precepts). You don't have to be a genius to develop a sound marketing plan. When it comes to marketing, you don't have to go the traditional route and it's not necessary to spend a lot of money (although it's so easy to do so). The following sections contain numerous suggestions on promotion, advertising and public relations. I recommend you get together with a few colleagues and brainstorm potential marketing techniques. Use the ideas presented in this book as a springboard for creativity.

• PROMOTION •

Promotion involves the activities and materials you produce to publicize your business. Some of the most effective means of promoting your practice are: networking (see page 30), making public presentations (lectures, free introductory seminars and demonstrations, conference booths, etc.), writing articles, sending direct mail pieces (letters of introduction, announcements and newsletters), obtaining referrals (see page 29), donating your services and having fabulous printed materials.

PRINTED MATERIALS —

Printed materials fall under the category of promotion because even though they cost you money to produce you don't have to pay a fee to distribute them. In most instances healing arts practitioners don't directly get clients from their printed materials (unless it's for a seminar, etc.). Clients tend to book sessions as a result of a personal interaction with the practitioner or from a referral. Thus, printed materials serve mainly as a reminder.

Business cards and brochures are the two most commonly used printed materials. For your visual promotional materials to be effective, they must appeal to the clients you want to attract — which might not necessarily be the layout that you personally like the best. (For specific tips on design, please see page 27.)

In the very least, you must have a substantial quantity of professional business cards. Choose a card that reflects who you are and the type of work you do. Always carry lots of business cards wherever you go. Keep extra cards in your car (or alternate method of transportation). Be generous with your promotional materials. The whole purpose is to circulate them, not hold onto them. Whenever you pass out your cards, always hand out at least three per person.

Although most of your printed materials are given out by you, your friends, colleagues and clients, it's still a worthwhile idea to post your cards and/or brochures in appropriate locations. Put them in health clubs, well-being centers, medical care supply shops, health food stores, offices of other health care practitioners, bookstores and places that the people in your target(s) frequent.

ARTICLES —

The written word is a powerful tool and it can immensely effect your business as well as your profession. In this field, education is the core of promotion. We have to enlighten the general public. They need to be informed of the scope of this field and the options available for their well-being.

Local newspapers and publications are always interested in information that is beneficial to their readership. Write an article on general health care, the value of your particular area of expertise or the latest innovations in your field. Don't worry about whether or not it's written perfectly — that's the job of the editor. I also recommend that you submit your articles to magazines and trade journals. You just never know who might be interested in what you have to say. Another option is to hire a professional journalist to write an article for you.

Articles build your credibility. Whether or not your articles get published, use them as promotional tools. Send them to your current clients and make them available to prospective clients.

PUBLIC PRESENTATIONS —

You are the best "method" of promotion for your practice. You are the reason people utilize your services. As long as you are in business it's wise to maintain a visible profile in your community. Make certain you do some type of public presentation at least once per month, and increase that to once per week if you are in the building phase of your practice. (For specific techniques on presentation skills, please refer to Chapter Three.)

Don't wait to be asked to speak. Contact the civic clubs, professional societies and networking associations whose members are likely to be prospective clients. Offer to give a lecture or demonstration. These organizations are forever on the lookout for speakers. Also, approach the local radio and cable television stations. They too are always in need of guests. Doing radio interviews are actually a lot of fun, particularly the call-in shows. Whenever you do a radio interview or make a cable TV appearance, be sure to tape it yourself since they don't always provide you with a copy of the show.

Set up regular introductory seminars and demonstrations. Hold monthly events at your office if the space is appropriate. An alternative is to have an organization (e.g., a teaching institution) sponsor your talks. You can even ask your clients to host them. If you are uncomfortable with giving seminars and demonstrations, find a colleague and do it together. It will be less stressful for you and provide your audience with a broader range of information and experience.

BOOTHS —

Another effective method for gaining visibility is to set up a booth at conferences, conventions and trade shows. You can meet a lot of people at these events. The following tips will assist in making this a productive experience.

- Be sure to have ample promotional materials available. You may want to print special fliers (much less expensive than brochures) for these events.

- Display your promotional materials in such a way that people will take them. This enables you to feel free to engage in a conversation with someone and not be concerned about missing potential clients.

- Although it's great to have an elaborate booth, don't let that be a deterrent. Do the best that you can within your budget. Just be sure to personalize it somehow with plants, photographs, or flowers, etc.

- Grab people's attention with an eye-catching sign. If you are unable to hang it up, put it on an easel.

- Provide ongoing demonstrations or give away product samples.

- Set out a bowl or basket to collect business cards. Put a sign in front of the bowl stating, "Enter here for a free drawing of...". If possible donate your services or products. If that's not appropriate, then give a prize (e.g., a book, a basket of healthy goodies or a gift certificate from a local store).

- Play a video tape that either demonstrates your services or gives interesting information (in an entertaining format).

- Bring necessary supplies. In addition to your promotional materials, make sure you have plenty of logistical supplies (e.g., equipment, masking tape, extension cords, pencils, paper, tissues), refreshments and clothing (in case you get cold, sweaty or spill something on yourself).

- Bring a friendly, knowledgeable person to help staff your booth. You need to be able to take breaks. It is imperative that you walk around and check out the other booths. Quite often, the best networking takes place between the booth owners.

DIRECT MAIL PIECES —

Direct mail pieces can be used as promotional tools to get new business as well as methods to retain current clients. They range from a formal letter of introduction to announcements to newsletters.

FORMAL LETTERS OF INTRODUCTION are an effective way to build your practice. Develop a strong network of associates by sending a letter of introduction to these allied professionals (e.g., physicians, counselors, chiropractors and other healing arts practitioners). Make sure the letter is typed and keep it to one page. Since most people don't like form mail, it's advisable to tailor each one for the particular individual. Do your homework and find out as much specific information as possible. Personalize your letters. You may even want to sign your letter in an ink that's a different color than the type (I tend to use a teal colored felt pen).

Direct the emphasis of your letter to the benefits of the reader. First introduce yourself and what you do — include your abilities and qualifications. Then focus on how you can help them, their practice and their clients. Next discuss the mutual benefits of your association. Close the letter by telling them how to contact you and advising them that you will be contacting them within the next two weeks. I recommend you also enclose your promotional material and an article that lends credence to your claims for potential benefits. After the letter has been sent, you must follow up.

ANNOUNCEMENTS are wonderful inexpensive promotional tools to enhance your visibility and keep you connected. Send out postcards to your current clients and choice prospective clients to announce special offers, speaking engagements and changes that occur in your practice (e.g., the addition of new staff, the incorporation of innovative techniques or equipment, or a change in status).

NEWSLETTERS are another powerful promotional medium that provide a great way to stay in touch, establish credibility and build rapport. People are more inclined to read something that is educational rather than promotional in nature. In designing a newsletter, make sure it's easy to read, conversational in tone and focuses on providing useful information. A newsletter need only be two pages long. Include sections on trends, quick tips and announcements about your business. If possible, incorporate photographs or some type of graphic illustration. Mail your newsletters on a quarterly (monthly is even better) basis. Don't confine your newsletters to your current clients. They also serve as a marketing tool for prospective clients.

DONATING YOUR SERVICES —

One of the easiest ways to gain visibility and promote your practice is to donate your services for fund-raising events. Target the appropriate groups according to your purpose (be it for professional advancement or personal gratification).

If your primary purpose is to promote your practice, choose events that are attended by people in your target market and/or those that are highly publicized. For major fund-raising events, make certain your donation is substantial enough to be considered one of the top prizes: this increases the likelihood of you being included in any publicity.

• ADVERTISING •

Advertising is gaining public notice for your business through means that require direct payment. Advertising venues include listings and display ads in publications, radio and TV commercials, signs and billboards and specialty advertising items such as pens embossed with your name or logo.

The steps in designing effective advertising are: Identify your target market, grab the audience's attention, highlight your differential advantage, list the benefits, state your offer, highlight the ad feature, request a response and provide a means of contact.

For advertising (particularly display) to be productive, it must be consistent. It is often wiser to place a smaller ad on a regular basis than to do a big splashy ad one time only.

MASS MEDIA advertising has typically been avoided by most healing arts practitioners, mainly due to the impersonal nature and the cost. This is starting to change. It is becoming more commonplace to hear ads on the radio, see billboards on the roads and even encounter television ads promoting health care practices. Yet most of these advertising techniques are usually employed by larger clinics rather than individual practitioners, or are announcing a specific event. Depending on the scope of your practice and your target market, you may find mass media advertising beneficial.

LISTINGS (often referred to as classified ads) tend to be the most productive form of advertising for healing arts practitioners. A listing is a concise, engaging description of your practice or announcement that is placed in a specific section of a publication. Classified ads are generally much less expensive than display ads — and you don't need to employ a commercial artist.

The major advantage of a listing is inherent in its definition. People look at listings because they are interested in what's being offered. Contrast this with display advertising in which you have to actually catch the attention of the reader.

To make sure your listing stands out, you must have a catchy headline. Other ways to increase the visibility of your listing is to put the headline in bold capital letters, bold the whole ad, include some type of graphic design or box the ad.

Places to put listings include the telephone yellow pages, business directories, trade journals, local publications, magazines, newsletters and special interest books.

SPECIALTY ADVERTISING ITEMS can be useful in any business. They are great promotional tools and make handy gifts. Check your local yellow pages for names of advertising specialty companies. Call them and request a catalog. The variety of these items is amazing. You can get almost anything personalized with your company name or logo! Choose items that will either directly remind your clients of you (or your specific services) or are of definite interest (or benefit) to the people in your target markets.

• PUBLIC RELATIONS •

Public relations is about keeping the public informed and interested in your business. It encompasses all the activities you do to obtain free media exposure for your business. Public relations is not advertising, although it can be significantly more effective. Public relations (henceforth PR) is a powerful, inexpensive tool for any business, yet people rarely take the time to work the system.

Some examples of PR are news releases, announcements, feature stories, interviews and press conferences. Networking and non-paid public speaking are also PR, yet they are generally considered promotional activities. Quite often you can you get free coverage of these activities in print or on the airwaves.

Advertising is distinguished from PR in that with the former, you must pay directly for your exposure. One of the areas where PR, advertising and promotion overlap has to do with calendar announcements in publications. Most newspapers and local magazines will give you a free listing for your event (even if you charge for it, e.g., a seminar).

The rest of this section focuses on press releases. Press releases play an integral part in effective public relations. It is the media's job to inform the public of newsworthy events. However, since they receive hundreds of press releases each week, you need to write your releases in a manner that catches the media's attention. Your odds of capturing an editor's interest in what you're doing (and saving your release from the trash bin) is greatly increased if s/he is able to quickly assess your release. Editors tend to take interest in things that are new, have magnitude, contain an element of human interest or are of benefit to the community.

Send out press releases on any major business changes and events. Don't worry about whether or not it's newsworthy. Let the editor be the judge. Your investment of a little time and postage can reap great rewards.

Presentation is crucial with press releases. Make certain they look good: typed, double-spaced on high quality paper (preferably letterhead) and that they conform to the preferred format standards (see following page). Keep your wording clear and conversational. Avoid using jargon. It is fine to use positive information about yourself, but steer clear of self-aggrandizement. For example, if your clientele has doubled due to a new promotion, added modalities, etc. — that's considered a newsworthy story. If you are the "first" to do something, back it up with facts.

Be sure that your sentences are simple and short. Make extensive use of paragraphs to clarify ideas. It works best to have your press release be only one page in length. If it is more than one page, follow these guidelines: type "(more)" at the bottom of each page — except on the last page; type "END", "30" or "###" after the final paragraph on the last page; and staple the pages together.

The press release format consists of source information, the release date, a headline, the body and the conclusion. On the following page is an example of how it would look on paper (the information in brackets "[ ]" is for illustrative purposes, not to be included in the actual release).

[Source Information]

Jan Smith
Health Unlimited
123 Breeze Way
Sea City, California 90000
(213) 555-5555

[Release Date]

For Immediate Release

[HEADLINE]

FREE WORKSHOP ON THE TEN STEPS TO STRESS REDUCTION

[Body]

Jan Smith, nationally known healing arts practitioner and trainer, will present a free stress reduction workshop Saturday, September 7th. The workshop is scheduled from 1 pm to 4 pm. It will be held at the Sea City Center at 456 Ocean Avenue.

Stress is a major contributing factor to a myriad of health problems. Learning how to relax is vital for your well-being. The techniques being demonstrated.... (This is where you would put other important details and supplemental information.)

[Conclusion]

To register for this workshop or receive information on stress reduction techniques, contact Jan Smith at 555-5555.

END

SOURCE INFORMATION

Name, company, address and phone number. Put this in the upper left corner of the page.

RELEASE DATE

If the story or announcement can be printed as soon as it's received, type "For Immediate Release". If you want it posted on a specific date, type "For Release, Monday, August 28". In general, it's best to have press releases that state "For Immediate Release". Otherwise you take the chance of an editor putting it aside and forgetting about it. Place the release date below the source information and to the right side of the page.

HEADLINE

This is a succinct summary of the content of the release. Word it in such a way that you put the information that would capture your reader's attention first — without making it sound like hype. Always type the headline in capital letters and underline it. Place the headline below the release date and flush with the left hand margin. Some examples of headlines are:

"FREE WORKSHOP ON INFANT MASSAGE"

"TERRY SMITH, SPORTS MASSAGE SPECIALIST, HAS JOINED TOUCH INC."

"DR. JONES TO DEMONSTRATE THE NEW PROCEDURES SHE LEARNED IN CHINA"

"PAUL REYNOLDS, LEADING HYPNOTHERAPIST, TO GIVE LECTURE ON STRESS REDUCTION"

BODY

The body contains the details about the release. The first paragraph should be a concise statement, expressing the most important features first. Cover who, what, where, why, when and how. Use separate paragraphs for additional information or supplemental material.

It is wise to use a multiple paragraph composition for the body because the space allotted for news stories and press releases constantly varies. This way, if by chance they have extra space and you've provided them ample material, they will use it. Also, if their space is limited, the vital information is easy for them to locate and use.

CONCLUSION

A separate paragraph indicating the action you want the reader, listener or viewer to take as a result of reading or hearing your story or announcement. You might type, "Call 555-5555 for more information" or "Stop by our Grand Opening on Saturday, August 28 from 10am-2pm".

After you have typed your press release, double check to make sure that you have included important dates, times and locations. Then proofread, proofread and proofread again. It is wise to have someone else proofread it as well.

When writing a press release, keep the purpose in mind. If you want to announce a new location, additional staff or an award, keep it simple and short. Some publications have a special section that highlights individuals or business in terms of being new, a change in status, relocation, staff additions, employee promotions and awards. These are usually only twenty words or less. So, if you know what you want it to say, don't make it too wordy lest you run the risk of the editor omitting crucial data. Also, include a photo.

If you want press coverage for an event, the release must spark interest. In this instance you would include an extra paragraph or so providing additional information.

Once you've prepared your press release, the next step is to distribute it properly. Send the release to a specific person. If you are unable to get the name, then address it to the relevant department (e.g., City Desk Editor or Calendar Editor).

Mail your releases so they are received at the appropriate time. Some publications have a deadline date of several months before the actual printing. Daily newspapers prefer lead time of at least one week in advance of the date you want the announcement to appear. If your release is very important, you may want to personally deliver it to the front desk of the publication's office.

Follow up your release with a telephone call. For events that you would like covered, contact the newspapers, radio and TV the day before or the morning of the event.

If you want to be interviewed, send a press kit. In this instance, definitely keep the release (which is in essence a cover letter) to one page. Include photos, supplemental information, articles about you, related articles (similar businesses, the benefits of your field of expertise, etc.), your brochure and your business card. Enclose these materials in a 9 x 12 envelope. Label the envelope "Press Kit" or "Media Kit", and then have it mailed or hand-delivered.

Whenever you get press coverage, send a thank-you note to the reporter who covered the story. It also never hurts to send a quick thank-you to the appropriate editors when your press releases get published. Acknowledgment is a fundamental element in building rapport and the higher it is, the more likely your next story will get the attention it deserves.

• DESIGNING VISUAL PROMOTIONAL PIECES •

Your visual promotional pieces reflect the character of your business. The ultimate design of your materials depends on your target market(s) and the image you wish to portray. Highlight your philosophy and differential advantage.

My own experience in preparing my printed materials leads me to recommend leaving it to the experts by hiring a graphic artist to do the job. If you are concerned about the cost, find an artist who is willing to barter services.

BUSINESS CARDS —

Design a business card that captures the essence of your practice. Remember that when it comes to cards, the beauty is in simplicity. A lot of controversy surrounds the amount and type of information to include on your card. Some people attempt to turn their business card into a brochure. In designing your cards, keep in mind that they aren't meant for you. They need to appeal to your **TARGET MARKET**.

Be very cautious about using logos. Avoid using one unless you are certain that you want to live with that symbol for a very long time. People tend to remember logos and associate you with your logo even if you no longer use that particular symbol. It is much easier to change a business name or image and alter the design or style of a card if it doesn't have a logo. It is best to wait until you are certain it's what you want. Also, it's advisable to check to see if anyone else has the same or similar one. Contact your Secretary of State for the requisite forms to trademark your logo.

BROCHURES —

Brochure design can be a bit more complicated. It is usually not wise to spend a lot of money on your first brochure since, invariably, you will want to alter it somehow. You may discover that the type style doesn't work well with the paper stock, someone points out an error, the perfect way to express yourself finally dawns on you or you find something you don't like.

When developing your brochure, remember that you must establish credibility and focus on the benefits. Techniques for establishing credibility in printed materials include providing credentials, numbers, lists, specific details, quotes, success stories, pictures and guarantees.

With unfortunate frequency, we describe ourselves (and our businesses) in terms of our features. But, a feature is not what attracts clients. They want to know how your services will make a difference in their well-being. For example, a feature is a description of: your service or product, how the product was made, the training received and the background of the practitioner and the company. Whereas a benefit is a description of: how the client will benefit from using the service and/or product, how the service/product will solve the client's problem, the differential advantage you provide and the results that the client can expect. If you decide to create your own brochure, purchase a book on effective brochure design.

BROCHURE DESIGN CRITERIA

- Does it easily distinguish who it's for?

- Does it identify with the target client's problem?

- Does it provide a solution to the problem?

- Does it appeal to the target client's needs?

- Does it have an interesting teaser?

- Are the lead benefits listed first?

- Is it believable?

- Is it attractive?

- Is it easy to read? Does it flow?

- Does it have sufficient white space?

- Are the type sizes and styles easy to read?

- Does it have appropriate photographs?

- Is it written in common language?

- Does it establish credibility?

- Is your address included?

- Does it include a map of your location?

- Does it include contact names and numbers?

- Does it provide a call for action?

REDUCING COSTS

Whether you design your own printed promotional materials or elect to utilize the services of a graphic artist, follow these tips for reducing your print media costs:

- Use interns from local colleges

- Barter for services

- Get at least three bids

- Use standard size and weight paper

- Use a photocopier for short print runs

- Print samples before using expensive paper & ink

- Use the printing services of trade and vocational schools

- Reuse effective material (as long as it's not being sent to the same people)

• THE REFERRAL PROCESS •

Frequently you hear that the healing arts is a word-of-mouth industry. Well, whose mouths are they anyway? You can not rely solely on your clients to build your practice. First of all, it's not their responsibility. And secondly, they may be uncomfortable telling others about their health care treatment. Your clients may not mention you unless someone asks. Creating a sound referral base takes a lot of attention and nurturing.

REQUEST THE REFERRAL —

First of all, you must directly ask for the referrals. Talk with your most satisfied clients. Ask them to support your business by telling their friends and colleagues about you. Supply them with business cards and other promotional material that they can hand out.

REPEAT THE REQUEST —

The next time you talk with them, repeat the request. People don't always hear things the first time. They may have been preoccupied (or if it was right after a session, they may have been too relaxed for the request to sink in). Ask them if they need more promotional material. Send them a thank-you note — even if you haven't gotten any clients from them. Thank them for their intention and support. They could be talking you up a storm, and you might never know it. They don't have control over whether or not the people they talk to call you to set up an appointment. Everyone likes to be acknowledged and knowing that you appreciate their efforts can inspire them to continue referring people to you. After a couple of weeks have passed, you can call them to find out if they have talked to anyone yet. Thank them again and ask them if there's anything you can do to help them promote you.

REWARD THE REFERRAL —

When you do get a referral, immediately send a thank-you note to the responsible party. Depending on the relationship you have with this person, you also may want to send him/her flowers, offer a free session or take him/her out to lunch or dinner. Whatever you do, don't send money! Your clients aren't salespeople on a commission.

RECIPROCATE THE REFERRAL —

Finally, it's imperative that you reciprocate. When someone refers a client to you, then go out of your way to either refer another client back or use his/her services and products yourself.

Remember, when it comes to promotion, the most important mouth is your own. Make yourself visible in your community. Be willing to speak about yourself at all times. Join business groups and leads clubs, attend public events, give free introductory seminars, write articles for your local papers, submit press releases and get on the public speaking circuit. Ultimately, you are the best advertisement for your business! The next section is an excellent example of making your presence known.

• NETWORKING •

Establishing a strong network is a fundamental for success in this field. Since so much of our business comes from word-of-mouth (referrals from clients, friends and other networking associates), it's crucial to begin fostering these associations immediately!

Networking is essentially a group of interconnected or cooperating individuals who develop and share contacts, information and support. An effective network is composed of many different types of people: people from whom you get information, experts whose services you utilize and can refer to others, people who keep you informed of events and opportunities, role models, people who are genuinely concerned about you and listen to you and support you, mentors, and people who actively refer potential clients to you.

Networking is actually a process, it's giving and receiving support. You can network informally by sharing resources with the people you come into contact with or formally by joining a networking group(s). It is important to remember that networking is composed of many skills that you must continue to develop and refine. The most successful networkers are those who actively support others in making connections. Networking is a wonderful example of the adage that the more you give, the more you receive.

The first step in enhancing your networking abilities is to recognize the vast potential for making connections for yourself and others. Whenever you meet someone, write down a few notes about them: where and when you met, who introduced you, what line of business they are in, what their interests are and what types of resources do they have, etc. Think about the other people you know to see if it would be beneficial for them to meet each other. Even if you are unable to make any connections right away, you may be able to do so in the future. You never know when a contact will come in handy.

The next step is to actually build your network. First of all, get a professional address book or card filing system for keeping track of your contacts. Include all pertinent information on each person and then keep it current. You may want to cross-index your files. When you collect business cards, always get at least three: one to file by name, one to file by business or occupation and one to give away (which ties into why you should always give out three of your cards). Become visible in your community by attending business, civic and social events, and joining professional and networking associations. Take seminars and classes. Be sure to attend various types of functions so that you can widen the scope of people you meet.

The last step (albeit a lifelong one) is to work your network. Follow up on leads and information with a phone call or note. Take the initiative. Always thank people that help you (either by giving you their time, support, advice, leads or contacts) even if you are not able to use their help or if the leads don't work out. When you are given a recommendation to utilize someone's services, tell the person who it was that gave you his/her name. When you give out referrals, make note of who you referred to whom. Then find out if the referral was successful. Be a giver and a receiver. Maintain contact with people in your network. Know what is happening. People's lives are constantly changing so it's important for you to periodically reassess your needs, priorities and contacts so you can be able to review your networking files and make appropriate connections. Add at least two people per month to your active network to keep it thriving. Finally, the most fundamental element in effective networking is to follow through on your commitments.

Networking Tips —

- Periodically reassess your needs, priorities and contacts.

- Have a professional address book or Rolodex. Keep it current.

- Collect business cards. On the back of the card write the date, where you met the person, who introduced you and any other specific information you want to remember.

- When you give out referrals, make note of who you referred to whom. Then find out if the referral was successful.

- Follow up initial meetings with a phone call or a note. Take the initiative. Everyone likes to know that people are interested in them.

- Maintain contact with people in your network. Know what is happening.

- Add at least 2 people per month to your active network.

- Join professional associations.

- Develop your own personal, professional and/or educational support groups.

- Attend workshops.

- Always take plenty of business cards to networking events and keep them in an easily accessible spot.

- Share your resources and contacts.

- Attend community functions.

- Always thank people that help you (either by giving you their time, support, advice, leads or contacts.). Be a giver and a receiver.

- Follow through on your commitments.

- Actively cultivate your current network and begin increasing it today.

Choosing a Networking Group —

It is essential for your professional and personal well-being to belong to at least one networking organization. Numerous types of networking groups exist from monthly social clubs, to community groups such as the Chamber of Commerce, to weekly "needs and leads" business associations. Participate in functions where you meet people with whom mutually beneficial relationships can be developed.

To determine which organization is best for you, first assess your needs and clarify your purpose and goals for networking in general. Ascertain the types of contacts you desire and appraise the assets you have to offer others. Then decide your purpose and goals for each specific group you are considering joining. You may want to become a member of one group mainly as a means for getting clients and join another association because you strongly support their goals and activities. You may decide to become part of an organization for the educational and informational opportunities, or join a club to make new friends and have fun. Sometimes one organization can meet several of your criteria.

The next step is to go to one or two meetings as a guest. Get a feel for the group. Notice whether or not you share any common interests and goals. Ask to see their bylaws and mission statement. If they don't have anything written, talk to several members and get feedback on their impressions of the group's purpose and philosophy. Find out the types of businesses and professions represented by the membership. Many organizations have a substantial membership fee, so it's wise to do some research before joining to determine if it's the right group for you.

Effective networking can be exciting and rewarding personally as well as financially! Become active in at least one business association and invest time in building your network of contacts and refining your networking skills.

Networking Group Checklist —

Assess Your Needs and Goals

- Determine the type(s) of groups that would be in alignment

Research Potential Groups

- What is the group's purpose (mission statement)?

- What year was it established?

- When does it meet, duration and location?

- What are the dues and fees?

- How many total members?

- How many active members?

- Number of members in your field?

- Types of businesses and professions represented?

Attend at Least Two Meetings

- Determine the group's philosophy

- See if you share any common interests and goals

TOOLS FOR EFFECTIVE FOLLOW-UP AND NETWORKING —

TICKLER FILES

Many people in all professions have found it useful to have some type of a "tickler" file. The purpose of such a device is to remind you of your commitments. It is a system designed to assist in your follow-through. Essentially, a tickler file contains 12 separate sections (one for each month) and a set of dividers numbered 1-31 (one for each day of the month). You can put these in a three-ring binder, an accordion file or hanging files. (Office supply stores carry a variety of these systems.) You put the 31 dividers in the Current Month Section. Then if someone asks you to contact them in two weeks, you go to your tickler file, turn to the corresponding date and make a note to call that person. Check your tickler file daily. Look at the current day and possibly the next two days. If you have a computer you can purchase planning software programs that include tickler systems. The true beauty of a tickler file is not so much in recording short-term information, but for keeping track of future events. For example, a client is going out of town for the summer and asks you to call back on September 12th. You put a note in the "September" section of your file. When it's the end of August and you are transferring your 31 dividers to September, you would put the note under the 12th. Using this system frees you from having to actively remember everything and helps ensure that you won't "forget" your commitments.

CONTACT/REFERRAL RECORDS

It is important to keep track of contacts and potential business resources. You may purchase predesigned forms or make your own sheets and put them in a binder with alphabetical dividers. It is recommended that you have a separate sheet for each person so that you can keep them in alphabetical order. Some of the information to include is the person's name, company, title, work address and phone number, home address and phone number, who referred you, where you met, any personal or professional information that you want, and action to be taken (see sample forms in Appendix A). Transfer the items from the action to be taken section to your tickler file and/or appointment book. You might also want to list the dates and times of any actions (telephone calls, meetings, etc.) that you make directly onto the contact form. This is particularly helpful as a document to record business interactions. For example, you get a bid for supplies over the phone and you place an order. Then you get your bill and it's for a different price. You are more likely to resolve the difference in your favor if you are able to say, "I talked with S. Smith on Tuesday, August 17th, at 3:20pm and was told...." The fact that you kept such precise records gives you more credibility.

Contact records also serve as a reminder. Review your contacts at least every two months. You may not have needed someone's services in the past, but as circumstances change your needs may change. Maybe you just met a person who could benefit from the services of someone in your contact files. Remember, networking isn't just fulfilling your needs but also assisting others in meeting their needs.

BUILDING AN EFFECTIVE NETWORK —

An effective network is composed of many different types of people. Please list below the names of the people that fit into each category (some names may be repeated since people often have more than one role in your life).

Who are the people from whom you get information?

_____

_____

_____

Who are the people who actively refer potential clients to you?

_____

_____

_____

List the experts whose services you use and can refer to others:

_____

_____

_____

Who keeps you informed of events and opportunities?

_____

_____

_____

List the people who are genuinely concerned about you, listen to you and support you:

_____

_____

_____

Who are your mentors?

_____

_____

_____

List your role models:

_____

_____

_____

Now that you have specified the people in your current network, please review the lists. Do one or two people perform most of the roles? Are there any areas that are lacking names? Are most of the people the same "type"? How do you feel about your network?

What kinds of support would you like to have right now?

_____

_____

_____

What additional types of support do you need over the next year?

_____

_____

_____

Who would you like to add to your network?

_____

_____

_____

On the following lines create at least ten goals for improving your network:

_____

_____

_____

_____

_____

_____

_____

_____

_____

_____

_____

"To make your networking work for you, you must work your network."
Donna Reed, President of Resources For Women, Inc.

— DECIDE TO NETWORK —

Decide to Network

Use every letter you write

Every conversation you have

Every meeting you attend

To express your fundamental beliefs and dreams

Affirm to others the vision of the world you want

Network through thoughts

Network through action

Network through love

Network through the spirit

You are the center of a network

You are the center of the world

You are a free, immensely powerful source

of life and goodness

Affirm it

Spread it

Radiate it

Think night and day about it

And you will see a miracle happen:

the greatness of your own life.

In a world of big powers, media, and monopolies

But of four and a half billion individuals

Networking is the new freedom

the new democracy

a new form of happiness.

— Robert Muller

• CLIENT RETENTION •

I have included this information on client retention in the marketing chapter because all too often we forget to market ourselves to our PRESENT clients. On the average, it costs six times as much money and it takes three times the effort getting a new client as retaining a current one. Yet, most people (particularly those that have been in business for more than two years) end up taking their clients for granted and focus their energy on obtaining new clients.

CUSTOMER SERVICE PRINCIPLES —

For those of you who have been in practice for a while, reflect upon your interactions with your clients. Are you still going out of your way to provide those "extra touches" — those actions above and beyond the actual work you do with your clients, or have you begun to take a less active role in customer service?

Business relations are similar to personal relationships. They both need attention and nurturing. It takes time, energy and a little creative thinking to foster goodwill and make your clients feel appreciated. For those of you who are concerned about your creative abilities, fear not, for I have included examples to spark your imagination.

Client retention is also a major concern for those in the process of transitioning from being a student to a certified practitioner. Shifting practicum clients to paying clients can be quite awkward. These people have been accustomed to paying a negligible fee (tip) for your services. Upon graduation, you may lose many of them if they are abruptly required to double or triple that amount. You can ease the discomfort by devising a method for gradually bringing them up to the rates you want to charge. For instance, let's say that you've determined your rate for a one-hour session will be $30.00. Several weeks before graduation, inform your current practicum clients of the rates you will be charging. Then tell them that you want to acknowledge them for their support (while you were a student) by charging them a modest fee and slowly increasing the cost till they are at your current rate. After graduation, you might start at $15.00 per session for the first three months, then increase your rates by $5.00 every three months until they are brought up to the rate you charge your other clients.

Once you have your clients, it's important that you take the steps necessary to keep them. Again, this is an example of how just being a fabulous healing arts practitioner is not enough. Whether or not you want to believe this, there are a lot of terrific practitioners out there, and the ones that have a steady clientele are the ones that also take the time and energy to do what is needed to retain their clients. The five major aspects of client retention are examined on the following pages. They are documentation, evaluations, motivation, follow-up and etiquette.

CLIENT RETENTION TECHNIQUES —

DOCUMENTATION is the foundation of client retention. You must know about your clients. Your records have to be accurate and complete. Most of your documentation will be in the form of client files. (Please refer to Chapter Four.) Be sure to review each client's file before you see him/her. Periodically review all of your files and sort them according to active and inactive status.

EVALUATIONS are another step in client retention. Periodically, have your clients rate you, your work and the results. This is a good source of feedback for you — it lets you know what areas you need to improve, plus it alerts you to what is important to each of your clients. The other benefit of evaluations is it gets the clients involved and responsible for their results.

MOTIVATION is one of the most difficult aspects in client retention. Technically you can't motivate anyone else, they have to motivate themselves. But there are some techniques to perk others' interest. One thing you can do is get your clients actively involved by having them create long term goals. Discuss your treatment plans with them — get their input. Educate your clients. Let them know where to locate information and products. Send them away with things such as articles, a copy of their goals, photos, samples, etc.

Many practitioners use a wonderful technique for rewarding their current clients while securing new clients at the same time by offering a free session to clients who refer three new people. It's a great application of Win/Win. You have to decide what techniques work best for you, keeping in mind that each client has his/her own idiosyncrasies.

FOLLOW-UP is the most forgotten and most vital step in client retention. It is a good business practice to call and remind new clients about their appointments. Some practitioners do this with all of their clients. Whenever you have a new client and/or a client that is going through major changes, it's recommended that several days after the session ask how your client is feeling. Get feedback. Let your client know that you are interested in his/her well-being. You may want to get permission (ahead of time) to call since some clients might not want to be contacted. Also, let your clients know that they can call you (subject to your policies).

You may choose to phone all of your clients after each session, particularly if you are in a building phase of your business. Send cards to your clients on holidays and other important dates such as birthdays and anniversaries. You may want to design a newsletter that you mail to all of your clients being sure to include copies of interesting articles. Always send thank-you notes for referrals. Also, it's okay to call a client if you haven't heard from them in a while. Oftentimes people get so caught up in their lives that they forget to take care of themselves and don't set up an appointment. They usually appreciate it when you call. Follow-up is about positioning — keeping yourself in your client's active memory.

ETIQUETTE mainly refers to your behavior with your clients. Since the standards for ethics and practices vary greatly (if they exist at all) within the different branches of the healing arts field, please realize that to your clients, you symbolize all practitioners. Treat your clients well during each session. Be considerate. When in doubt about anything, ask questions. Don't ever make assumptions. Not all of your clients are going to be outgoing and communicative. Let your client know that you honor his/her privacy and that what happens during the session is held in total confidence (subject to local laws), and then keep that confidence. Respect your clients — even though you may not necessarily agree with their viewpoints. Not everyone shares the same beliefs about exercise, nutrition and health in general. It is one thing to offer information and support, but it's totally inappropriate to attempt to enforce your belief systems on your clients.

Every time you see a client, treat him/her as though this is your first session — remember with each interaction, you are making a new first impression. Greet your client appropriately. Granted, if this is his/her fourth appointment, you will probably be less formal (yet still show the same amount of concern) than you were the first time you met. Your greeting sets the tone for the entire session and can be the determining factor in whether or not the client returns.

Flexibility is the key to good client relations. For example, you may feel that your sessions are more effective done one way, and yet some clients prefer an alternative method. You must take the client's style into consideration.

Observe your clients' likes and dislikes. If you know a client likes to have a particular little thing done, do it. Or perhaps s/he really prefers to have a session on a particular day — do your best to appropriately arrange your schedule. Take the time to pay attention to those details. Go that extra step. Your clients will be very appreciative. For example, a massage therapist may offer to wipe the oil off of a client with astringent and put a shower cap or towel over the client's hair to avoid getting it oily. A counselor may have a mat available in case a client wants to be able to move around. A physician might warm up the stethoscope — particularly on cold days....

All healing arts practitioners need to be aware of their clients' state after each session. Allow your clients time to reorient and offer to help them get up. You might also offer your clients something to drink (water, juice or tea) before or at the end of a session. These are just a few examples of going that extra step. Not every client has the same wants and needs. You need to make yourself aware. In summary, it's important to record and remember the "little things" and do them!

— THE CLIENT —

... IS THE MOST IMPORTANT PERSON IN OUR BUSINESS.

... IS THE REASON FOR OUR WORK, NOT AN INTERRUPTION.

... IS DOING US A FAVOR BY PURCHASING OUR SERVICES AND GOODS.

... IS A FEELING HUMAN BEING.

... IS SOMEONE THAT WANTS A BREAK — TO BE TAKEN CARE OF.

... IS THE PERSON WHO ENABLES US TO EARN AN INCOME.

... IS DESERVING OF THE BEST SERVICE WE CAN OFFER.

CHAPTER SIX

THE BUSINESS PLAN

THE BUSINESS PLAN _____

• INTRODUCTION •

A business plan serves many functions. It is the foundation for a thriving business. It is a powerful declaration of your goals and intentions. A business plan is a written summary of what you aim to accomplish and how you intend to organize your resources to attain those goals. Developing an effective business plan generally requires a considerable amount of time. You have to do a lot of honest thinking in addition to some technical research. A business plan addresses these issues: What are you offering? Who will be your clients? What needs are your services satisfying? How will your potential clients find you? How much money do you plan on making? and What actions do you intend on taking to ensure success?

The major components of a business plan are a description of the business, long range and short term goals, a financial forecast and a marketing plan. A business plan can be used as a motivational tool for keeping you on track. This is important since it can be so easy to get caught up in day-to-day working that you don't take the time to plan the strategies to ensure future success, or get overwhelmed and miss other potential opportunities.

Having a business plan as a reference can keep you focused. Putting down how and what you want, encourages you to be more realistic. It also assists you in anticipating problems so that you can possibly avoid them or at least be prepared so that you can overcome them — thus minimizing your risks. Having clearly stated goals gives you a basis for evaluating progress. In creating a business plan you become aware of the finances that are really required to start and maintain a thriving business.

Also, the odds of getting a loan from a bank are greatly increased if you submit a typed business plan. You will be perceived as a lower risk because you have demonstrated that you do have some business savvy.

Finally, by developing a business plan you may discover steps vital to your success and happiness that you may have otherwise been unaware of or overlooked.

The majority of work you have been doing thus far has been to set the stage for your business plan. The rest of this section is a worksheet version for outlining a business plan. Before you start, scan through it first. This will provide you with a sense of the direction and scope of the plan. After you have reviewed the worksheets, fill out each section. You already have some of the necessary information from the exercises in the previous chapters. Use this outline to refine what you have already written and to clarify the other details that are requisites to your success.

• OWNER'S STATEMENT •

A one page description of the business and the owner.

Business Name: _____

_____

Business Address: _____

_____

Business Phone: _____

Owner's Name: _____

_____

Owner's Home Address: _____

_____

Owner's Home Phone: _____

Brief Business Description:

Include how long the business has been established, list the services offered and summarize your business experience and philosophy.

_____

_____

_____

_____

_____

_____

_____

Statement of Current Business Financial Status:

_____

_____

_____

_____

_____

_____

_____

• OVERVIEW •

A one page summation of the highlights of the business plan.*

_____

_____

_____

_____

_____

_____

_____

_____

_____

_____

_____

_____

_____

_____

_____

_____

_____

_____

_____

_____

_____

_____

_____

_____

_____

_____

* Do this after the other sections of the business plan have been completed.

• PURPOSE, PRIORITIES AND GOALS •

A detailed description of your career plan. Refer to the goals you've written in Chapter Two.

A. OVERALL CAREER —

State your purpose and at least six priorities for your career.

_____

_____

_____

_____

_____

_____

_____

_____

B. LONG RANGE —

State your long range (3-5 year) purpose, at least six priorities and at least two goals per priority for your career.

_____

_____

_____

_____

_____

_____

_____

_____

_____

_____

_____

_____

_____

_____

C. Short Term —

List your short term (1-2 year) purpose, at least six priorities and at least three goals per priority for your career.

_____

_____

_____

_____

_____

_____

_____

_____

_____

_____

_____

_____

_____

_____

_____

_____

_____

_____

_____

_____

_____

_____

_____

_____

_____

_____

_____

• DEFINITION OF THE BUSINESS •

A description of your services and possible products.

A. DESCRIBE YOUR LOCATION(S) —

_____

_____

_____

_____

_____

_____

B. DEFINE (IN DETAIL) THE MAJOR SERVICES OFFERED —

_____

_____

_____

_____

_____

_____

C. LIST OTHER SERVICES OFFERED —

_____

_____

_____

_____

_____

_____

D. LIST SPECIAL PRODUCTS USED —

_____

_____

_____

_____

_____

_____

E. List All Equipment Used —

_____

_____

_____

_____

_____

_____

F. Unique Features —

Describe the unique features that distinguish your practice from others: Include attributes such as experience, variety of services/techniques, pricing, location, outcalls, product sales, equipment, supplies, credit terms, management abilities and capital.

_____

_____

_____

_____

_____

_____

_____

_____

_____

_____

_____

G. Product Sales —

If selling products — define your position in the chain of distribution, list the types of suppliers (or names) that you buy from and specify the types of clients that purchase products.

_____

_____

_____

_____

_____

_____

• MARKETING •

The foundation for creating a thriving client base.

A. OVERVIEW —

This section is about clarifying your beliefs and attitudes toward your profession and determining the image you wish to portray.

1. Describe the "character" that you want for your practice. Depict the image you want to convey:

_____

_____

_____

_____

_____

_____

_____

2. State your philosophy in regards to your profession:

_____

_____

_____

_____

_____

_____

_____

3. Describe your philosophy regarding your practice in particular:

_____

_____

_____

_____

_____

_____

_____

B. CLIENT PROFILE —

This is a descriptive analysis of your current and potential clients — who they are, what their interests are and where you can find them. Include each of your target markets.

1. Target Market 1:

_____

_____

_____

_____

_____

_____

_____

_____

_____

2. Target Market 2:

_____

_____

_____

_____

_____

_____

_____

_____

_____

3. Target Market 3:

_____

_____

_____

_____

_____

_____

_____

_____

_____

C. INCOME POTENTIAL —

Contact your professional society or several of the major teaching institutions (for your specific field) to get this information. You may have to do some informal research because this data has not been compiled for many professions.

1. Describe the existing business conditions. Where do you stand in the current "state of the art"?

_____

_____

_____

_____

_____

_____

2. Describe the projections and trends for your specific profession:
Nationally.

_____

_____

_____

Locally.

_____

_____

_____

3. List the average income for practitioners in your specific field:

	Nationally	Locally
The first six months.	$ _____	$ _____
The first year.	$ _____	$ _____
The second year.	$ _____	$ _____
The third year.	$ _____	$ _____

4. List the average total number of clients per practitioner:

	Nationally	Locally
The first six months.	_____	_____
The first year.	_____	_____
The second year.	_____	_____
The third year.	_____	_____

D. ATTRACTING CLIENTS —

This section is about creating strategies to inform people who you are — getting your share of the market.

1. List the differences and benefits of your business/practice (your Differential Advantage):

_____

_____

_____

_____

_____

_____

_____

_____

2. How will your potential clients recognize the difference?

_____

_____

_____

_____

_____

_____

_____

_____

3. What is your position statement?

_____

_____

_____

_____

_____

_____

_____

_____

4. List your rates:
By the hour, half-hour, session and series of sessions (e.g., 3 for $ __, 5 for $ __, 10 for $ __). Have your fee structure set in advance, including reduced rates for specific clientele (e.g., allied health care practitioners, students and special populations, etc.).

_____

_____

_____

_____

_____

_____

_____

_____

5. List the amenities to be absorbed in pricing:
Including credit offered, outcalls, parking, consultation, extended business hours, educational materials, samples and supplies.

_____

_____

_____

_____

_____

_____

_____

_____

6. Describe your competition's effect on pricing:

_____

_____

_____

_____

_____

_____

_____

_____

E. ANALYSIS OF YOUR COMPETITION —

Some ways to discover this information are to examine the yellow pages, request brochures, check the library for articles and actually utilize your competitors' services. (Refer to Marketing Chapter for more details.)

1. Number of practitioners in city. _____

2. Number of group practices. _____

3. Number of practitioners specializing in your area of expertise. _____

4. Number of practitioners within a three mile radius. _____

5. Names of your major competitors. Include the types of services offered, their strengths and weaknesses:

_____

_____

_____

_____

_____

_____

_____

_____

6. Weaknesses your business has in comparison to your competition:

_____

_____

_____

_____

_____

_____

_____

7. Steps you'll take to overcome those weaknesses:

_____

_____

_____

_____

_____

_____

_____

F. COMPETITION'S MARKETING ASSESSMENT —

The first phase in planning your promotional campaign is appraising the competition. List each of your major competitors and describe the marketing strategies they utilize. Be certain to include where and how often they advertise.

1. Major Competitor 1:

_____

_____

_____

_____

2. Major Competitor 2:

_____

_____

_____

_____

3. Major Competitor 3:

_____

_____

_____

_____

4. Major Competitor 4:

_____

_____

_____

_____

5. Major Competitor 5:

_____

_____

_____

_____

6. Major Competitor 6:

_____

_____

_____

_____

G. Promotion and Advertising Plan —

In designing your promotional plan, it's wise to use a variety of media. You must have specific goals, timelines and budgets for each marketing application. (Refer to Chapter Five.)

1. Marketing your services:

Media	Goal	Timeline	Budget
_____	_____	_____	_____
_____	_____	_____	_____
_____	_____	_____	_____
_____	_____	_____	_____
_____	_____	_____	_____
_____	_____	_____	_____
_____	_____	_____	_____
_____	_____	_____	_____
_____	_____	_____	_____
_____	_____	_____	_____
_____	_____	_____	_____
_____	_____	_____	_____
_____	_____	_____	_____
_____	_____	_____	_____
_____	_____	_____	_____
_____	_____	_____	_____
_____	_____	_____	_____
_____	_____	_____	_____
_____	_____	_____	_____
_____	_____	_____	_____
_____	_____	_____	_____
_____	_____	_____	_____
_____	_____	_____	_____
_____	_____	_____	_____

2. If you sell products, include a description and cost for:

a. Inside displays:

_____

_____

_____

_____

_____

b. Additional sales staff (include training):

_____

_____

_____

_____

_____

c. Equipment:

_____

_____

_____

_____

_____

d. Special promotions, discounts, etc:

_____

_____

_____

_____

3. Promotional budget per year

   a. Total cost of media: $ _____

   b. Total cost for product promotion: $ _____

   c. Total promotional budget: $ _____

   d. Cost per potential client: $ _____

4. Outline your marketing plan (this may take several pages) in a timeline format:

GOAL	TARGET DATE
_____	_____
_____	_____
_____	_____
_____	_____
_____	_____
_____	_____
_____	_____
_____	_____
_____	_____
_____	_____
_____	_____
_____	_____
_____	_____
_____	_____
_____	_____
_____	_____
_____	_____
_____	_____
_____	_____
_____	_____
_____	_____
_____	_____
_____	_____
_____	_____
_____	_____
_____	_____
_____	_____
_____	_____

5. How will your marketing strategies enable you to succeed?

_____

_____

_____

_____

_____

_____

_____

_____

_____

_____

_____

_____

_____

6. What are some of the areas that require special attention?

_____

_____

_____

_____

_____

_____

_____

_____

_____

_____

_____

_____

_____

• CLIENT INTERACTION POLICIES •

A set of guidelines for you and your clients.

A. YOUR REQUIREMENTS OF THE CLIENT —

Items to consider are: scheduling, promptness and cancellation policies; honesty and communications; hygiene; fee structure and payment methods; and refund policies.

_____

_____

_____

_____

_____

_____

_____

_____

_____

_____

_____

B. WHAT YOUR CLIENT CAN EXPECT FROM YOU —

Include your style, scheduling, cancellation policy, availability (consultations/support by telephone and in person) and as a source of educational information, etc....

_____

_____

_____

_____

_____

_____

_____

_____

_____

_____

• FINANCIAL FORECAST •

A statement of your current status and a forecast for the next 12 months.

OPENING BALANCE SHEET —
    Date: _____

— ASSETS —

CURRENT ASSETS
    Cash and bank accounts $ _____

    Accounts receivable $ _____

    Inventory $ _____

    Other current assets $ _____

      TOTAL CURRENT ASSETS   **(A)** $ _____

FIXED ASSETS
    Property owned $ _____

    Furniture and equipment $ _____

    Business automobile $ _____

    Leasehold improvements $ _____

    Other fixed assets $ _____

      TOTAL FIXED ASSETS   **(B)** $ _____
      TOTAL ASSETS   **(A+B=X)** $ _____

— LIABILITIES —

CURRENT LIABILITIES (DUE WITHIN NEXT 12 MONTHS)
    Bank loans $ _____

    Other loans $ _____

    Accounts payable $ _____

    Other current liabilities $ _____

      TOTAL CURRENT LIABILITIES   **(C)** $ _____

LONG-TERM LIABILITIES
    Mortgages $ _____

    Long-term loans $ _____

    Other long-term liabilities $ _____

      TOTAL LONG-TERM LIABILITIES   **(D)** $ _____
      TOTAL LIABILITIES   **(C +D = Y)** $ _____
      NETWORTH   **(X - Y = Z)** $ _____
      TOTAL NET WORTH AND LIABILITIES   **(Y + Z)** $ _____

Business Income and Expense Forecast For The Next 12 Months —

One year estimate ending _____ , 19 _____

— PROJECTED NUMBER OF CLIENTS —

For your services _____

For your products _____

TOTAL NUMBER OF CLIENTS _____

— PROJECTED INCOME —

Sessions $_____

Product sales $_____

Other $_____

TOTAL INCOME (A) $_____

— PROJECTED EXPENSES —

Start-up costs $_____

Monthly expenses (x 12) $_____

Annual expenses $_____

TOTAL EXPENSES (B) $_____

TOTAL OPERATING PROFIT (OR LOSS) (A - B) $_____

CAPITAL REQUIRED FOR THE NEXT 12 MONTHS $_____

START-UP COSTS WORKSHEET —

ITEM	ESTIMATED EXPENSE
Open Checking Account	$ _____
Telephone Installation	$ _____
Equipment	$ _____
First & Last Month's Rent, Security Deposit, etc.	$ _____
Supplies	$ _____
Business Cards, Stationery, etc.	$ _____
Advertising & Promotion Package	$ _____
Decorating & Remodeling	$ _____
Furniture & Fixtures	$ _____
Legal & Professional Fees	$ _____
Insurance	$ _____
Utility Deposits	$ _____
Beginning Inventory	$ _____
Installation of Fixtures and Equipment	$ _____
Licenses and Permits	$ _____
Other	$ _____
TOTAL	$ _____

FIXED ANNUAL EXPENSE WORKSHEET —

ITEM	ESTIMATED EXPENSE
Property Insurance	$ _____
Business Auto Insurance	$ _____
Licenses and Permits	$ _____
Liability Insurance	$ _____
Disability Insurance	$ _____
Professional Society Membership	$ _____
Fees (legal, accounting, etc.)	$ _____
Taxes	$ _____
Other	$ _____
TOTAL	$ _____

Monthly Business Expense Worksheet —

EXPENSE	ESTIMATED MONTHLY COST	x 12
Rent	$ 200	$ 2,400
Utilities	$ 0	$ 0
Telephone	$ 50	$ 600
Bank fees	$ 7	$ 84
Supplies	$ 20	$ 240
Stationery & Business Cards	$ 10	$ 120
Networking club dues	$ —	$ —
Education (seminars, books, professional journals, etc.)	$ 80	$ 960
Business Car (payments, gas, repairs, etc.)	$ —	$ —
Advertising & Promotion	$ —	$ —
Postage	$ 7	$ 84
Entertainment	$ —	$ —
Repair, Cleaning & Maintenance	$ 10	$ 120
Travel	$ —	$ —
Business Loan Payments	$ 100	$ 1200
Salary/Draw*	$ 1500	$ 18000
Staff Salaries	$ —	$ —
Miscellaneous Insurance	$ 17	$ 200
Taxes	$ 660	$ 7920
Professional Fees	$ 17	$ 204
Decorations	$ 10	$ 120
Furniture & Fixtures	$ —	$ —
Equipment	$ 20	$ 240
Inventory	$ —	$ —
Other Savings	$ 250	$ 3000

TOTAL MONTHLY $ 2,958

TOTAL YEARLY $ 35,492

In most instances it is not wise or appropriate to take draw for the first 6-12 months.

Personal Budget Estimates For The Next Twelve Months —

		Estimated Monthly Cost	x 12
INCOME			
Income (draw) from business		$ 1,500	$ 18,000
Income from other sources		$ 2,600	$ 31,200
TOTAL INCOME		$ 4,100	$ 49,200
EXPENSES			
Rent	325	$ 450	$ 5400
Home Insurance	—	$ —	$ —
Health Insurance	—	$ —	$ —
Utilities	200	$ 200	$ 2400
Telephone	100	$ 100	$ 1200
Auto:			
payments	—	$ 300	$ 3600
gas	160	$ 160	$ 1920
maintenance	25	$ 50	$ 600
insurance	85	$ 85	$ 1020
other	—	$ —	$ —
Food	200	$ 200	$ 2400
Household Supplies	—	$ —	$ —
Clothing		$ 100	$ 1200
Laundry/Dry Cleaning	—	$ —	$ —
Education	200	$ —	$ —
Entertainment	600	$ 600	$ 7200
Travel	—	$ —	$ —
Contributions	—	$ 500	$ 6000
Health	—	$ —	$ —
Home Repair and Maintenance		$ —	$ —
Self Development	—	$ —	$ —
Outstanding Loans and Credit Card Payments	—	$ —	$ —
Miscellaneous Expenses	100 / 2000	$ 100	$ 1200
TOTAL EXPENSES		$ 2845	$ 34,140
BALANCE (+/-)		$ +1255	$ +15,060

Cash Flow Forecast —

		JANUARY Est. Actual		FEBRUARY Est. Actual		MARCH Est. Actual	
BEGINNING CASH	$						
PLUS MONTHLY INCOME FROM:							
Fees	$						
Sales	$						
Loans	$						
Other	$						
TOTAL CASH AND INCOME	$						
EXPENSES:							
Rent	$						
Utilities	$						
Telephone	$						
Bank Fees	$						
Supplies	$						
Stationery & Business Cards	$						
Insurance	$						
Dues	$						
Education	$						
Auto	$						
Advertising & Promotion	$						
Postage	$						
Entertainment	$						
Repair & Maintenance	$						
Travel	$						
Business Loan Payments	$						
Licenses & Permits	$						
Salary/Draw	$						
Staff Salaries	$						
Taxes	$						
Professional Fees	$						
Decorations	$						
Furniture & Fixtures	$						
Equipment	$						
Inventory	$						
Other Expenses	$						
TOTAL EXPENSES	$						
ENDING CASH (+/-)	$						

Cash Flow Forecast —

	APRIL		MAY		JUNE	
	ESTIMATE	ACTUAL	ESTIMATE	ACTUAL	ESTIMATE	ACTUAL
BEGINNING CASH	$					

PLUS MONTHLY INCOME FROM:

Fees	$					
Sales	$					
Loans	$					
Other	$					
TOTAL CASH AND INCOME	$					

EXPENSES:

Rent	$					
Utilities	$					
Telephone	$					
Bank Fees	$					
Supplies	$					
Stationery & Business Cards	$					
Insurance	$					
Dues	$					
Education	$					
Auto	$					
Advertising & Promotion	$					
Postage	$					
Entertainment	$					
Repair & Maintenance	$					
Travel	$					
Business Loan Payments	$					
Licenses & Permits	$					
Salary/Draw	$					
Staff Salaries	$					
Taxes	$					
Professional Fees	$					
Decorations	$					
Furniture & Fixtures	$					
Equipment	$					
Inventory	$					
Other Expenses	$					
TOTAL EXPENSES	$					
ENDING CASH (+/-)	$					

CASH FLOW FORECAST —

	JULY		AUGUST		SEPTEMBER	
	ESTIMATE	ACTUAL	ESTIMATE	ACTUAL	ESTIMATE	ACTUAL
BEGINNING CASH	$					
PLUS MONTHLY INCOME FROM:						
Fees	$					
Sales	$					
Loans	$					
Other	$					
TOTAL CASH AND INCOME	$					
EXPENSES:						
Rent	$					
Utilities	$					
Telephone	$					
Bank Fees	$					
Supplies	$					
Stationery & Business Cards	$					
Insurance	$					
Dues	$					
Education	$					
Auto	$					
Advertising & Promotion	$					
Postage	$					
Entertainment	$					
Repair & Maintenance	$					
Travel	$					
Business Loan Payments	$					
Licenses & Permits	$					
Salary/Draw	$					
Staff Salaries	$					
Taxes	$					
Professional Fees	$					
Decorations	$					
Furniture & Fixtures	$					
Equipment	$					
Inventory	$					
Other Expenses	$					
TOTAL EXPENSES	$					
ENDING CASH (+/-)	$					

CASH FLOW FORECAST —

	OCTOBER		NOVEMBER		DECEMBER	
	ESTIMATE	ACTUAL	ESTIMATE	ACTUAL	ESTIMATE	ACTUAL
BEGINNING CASH $						
PLUS MONTHLY INCOME FROM:						
Fees $						
Sales $						
Loans $						
Other $						
TOTAL CASH AND INCOME $						
EXPENSES:						
Rent $						
Utilities $						
Telephone $						
Bank Fees $						
Supplies $						
Stationery & Business Cards $						
Insurance $						
Dues $						
Education $						
Auto $						
Advertising & Promotion $						
Postage $						
Entertainment $						
Repair & Maintenance $						
Travel $						
Business Loan Payments $						
Licenses & Permits $						
Salary/Draw $						
Staff Salaries $						
Taxes $						
Professional Fees $						
Decorations $						
Furniture & Fixtures $						
Equipment $						
Inventory $						
Other Expenses $						
TOTAL EXPENSES $						
ENDING CASH (+/-) $						

• OPERATIONS •

An overview of organization, procedures and policies.

A. MANAGEMENT QUALIFICATIONS —

1. What are the Management Qualifications needed to run the "business" part of your practice?

_____

_____

_____

_____

_____

_____

_____

_____

2. List necessary/desired qualities:

_____

_____

_____

_____

_____

_____

_____

_____

3. List any current limitations:

_____

_____

_____

_____

_____

_____

_____

_____

B. Group Practice —

1. Describe the various functions and the person(s) responsible:

_____

_____

_____

_____

2. What is the level of authority for each person? Include areas such as hiring, firing, scheduling and purchasing:

_____

_____

_____

_____

C. Company Policies —

1. Scheduling:

_____

_____

_____

2. Promotion:

_____

_____

_____

3. Client interaction:

_____

_____

_____

4. Operations:

_____

_____

_____

5. Legal agreements:

_____

_____

_____

D. PART-TIME STAFFING —

1. List functions and how many people for each function:

_____

_____

_____

_____

2. Describe the training they need:

_____

_____

_____

_____

3. Define your compensation plan:

_____

_____

_____

_____

E. MAINTENANCE AND SAFETY —

1. What are your security needs? Consider client screening, location safety and night travel.

_____

_____

_____

_____

_____

2. List your procedures for repairs, maintenance and cleaning:

_____

_____

_____

_____

_____

F. Equipment —

1. List equipment and supplies needed for next 12 months:

_____

_____

_____

_____

_____

2. Acquisition plan (buy or lease) and priority:

_____

_____

_____

_____

_____

3. Source of financing for equipment and supplies:

_____

_____

_____

_____

_____

G. Inventory Plan (for those who also sell products) —

1. Estimated inventory levels needed:

_____

_____

_____

_____

_____

2. Inventory technique(s) to be used:

_____

_____

_____

_____

H. ACCOUNTING AND CONTROL —

1. Who does the bookkeeping? (Self or other): _____

2. Management reports — frequency:

   a. Balance sheets. _____

   b. Condition of client accounts. _____

   c. Profit and loss statements. _____

   d. Expense reports. _____

   e. Forecasting. _____

   f. Service reports (e.g., number of clients/time per client) _____

   g. If selling products:

       1). Sales reports. _____

       2). Inventory reports. _____

3. Financial guidelines:

This section has to do with setting your parameters: debt limits and duration, the amount of money you want "tied up" in your business and the inventory turnover rate.

   a. Debt to capital limits: _____

   _____

   b. Average collection period for credit accounts: _____

   _____

   c. Return on your initial investment: _____

   _____

   d. Liquidity ratios: _____

   _____

   e. Product sales — inventory turns: _____

   _____

• SUCCESS STRATEGIES •

List your goals for developing your success strategies. Specify your methods for implementing your business plan and having a prosperous practice. Include activities such as: developing strategic plans, creating monthly flow charts, identifying decision points, reviewing and revising your plans, creating a business support system, networking and choosing appropriate advisors.

GOAL	TARGET DATE

• APPENDIX •

The types of additional information and/or documents (if any at all) to be included in this section depend upon the nature of your business plan. If your business plan is mainly for your personal use, you may not need to add anything else. But if you intend on using your business plan to obtain a business loan, consider including the following data. This list is only a guide. Check with the specific lending institutions to find out their requirements.

- Personal net worth statement.
- Copies of last two year's income statements and balance sheets.
- List of client commitments.
- Copies of business legal agreements.
- Credit status reports.
- News articles about you or your business.
- Copies of promotional material.
- Letters of recommendation from your clients.
- Personal references.

• SUPPLEMENT •

If your business plan is to be used in securing a loan, it's recommended to incorporate the following additional information to the previous sections of the business plan.

INCLUDE IN THE INTRODUCTION —

1. State the type of business loan(s) you're seeking (e.g., term loan, line of credit or mortgage).

2. Summarize the proposed use of the funds.

INCLUDE IN THE FINANCIAL FORECAST —

1. Calculate a break-even analysis. Determine at what client (or sales) volume your business will break even. This is the point where total costs equal total income. You may need to update this every few months in order to accurately reflect your business growth.

2. Describe the loan requirements: the amount needed, the terms and the date by which it's required.

3. State the purpose of the loan, detailing the facets of the business to be financed.

4. Provide a statement of the owner's equity.

5. List any outstanding loans. Include balance due, repayment terms, purpose of the loan and status.

6. Document your current operating line of credit — the amount and security held.

ADD A SECTION ON RISK ASSESSMENT —

1. Describe in detail the effects of your competition on all phases of your business.

2. List possible external events that might occur to hamper your success: a recession, new competition, shifts in client demand, unfavorable industry trends, problems with suppliers and changes in legislation.

3. Identify potential internal problems: income projections not realized, long term illness or serious injury.

4. Develop a contingency plan to counteract the most significant risks.

ADD A SECTION TITLED REFERENCES —

1. List all pertinent information regarding your current lending institution: branch, address, types of accounts and contact person.

2. List the names, addresses and phone numbers of your attorney, accountant and business consultant.

CHAPTER SEVEN

SELF MANAGEMENT

SELF MANAGEMENT

• INTRODUCTION •

Thriving on chaos — a phrase that Tom Peters has made so common in the market place — is also an apt description of the way many of us lead our lives. But what is the price of our success? Have we excised ourselves (and our families) from our lives? It is so easy to get enmeshed in our projects — telling ourselves that we will take time off next weekend, or maybe next month, well, at least sometime this year....

Quite often we have conflicting ideas of what it means to be successful and our requirements for success may vary greatly in the personal, business and social realms. Explore your values and how they relate to your success. Consider what it means to be successful: Are you successful only if you earn a certain amount of money, perform miracles in your work, look a particular way, are in a perfect relationship, drive a great car or live in the right neighborhood? In other words, what are your values? Is success a "thing" to be achieved or a way of being?

In the book *Lead, Follow or Get Out of the Way,* Jim Lundy describes success as the achievement of predetermined goals. This means any goal! The principal word is "predetermined." For instance, you may have accomplished something (possibly even something major) that you hadn't really intended or even given much thought to, and somehow the victory seemed hollow. Most likely that feeling was because you hadn't previously claimed it as a goal. (Please refer to Chapter Two.) Achievements are so much more fulfilling when they are planned. Thus, success is really a process — one that involves setting and achieving goals.

There is truly an art to being successful in the business world while staying balanced. This would be simple if our lives weren't filled with meaningful activities. Unfortunately, that just isn't the case. Most of us have a career/business, a family, social activities and civic responsibilities. And all of these are important. At times we may feel like we're jugglers in a circus — keeping everything going, yet not being able to fully enjoy any one aspect. So, what can be done? We certainly can't create a 30 hour day. The key lies in Self Management.

Self management is the ability to artfully direct your life so that you easily and joyfully accomplish what you desire. It is about increasing your personal productivity while staying true to yourself. Some of the components of effective self management include: time management, assessing your values (Chapter One) and operating from them, clarifying your purpose, priorities and goals (Chapter Two), risk-taking, tracking, self-motivation, balancing personal and professional priorities, overcoming your barriers to success, flexibility, choosing appropriate advisors, and the dedication to learning and self-improvement.

• BARRIERS TO SUCCESS •

Most of our barriers to success have been forged by our own hands. Self-sabotage is an all too common occurrence. Sometimes we do this in little ways and other times it becomes a way of life. This usually stems from negative conditioning (see Chapter One).

Typical manifestations of self-sabotage are: possessing a poor self image, blaming others for any misfortunes, expecting failure, putting yourself down (negative self-talk), repeating errors (not learning from past) and surrounding yourself with inappropriate people. The most common symptom of self-sabotage with the small business owner is procrastination.

"Never put off until tomorrow what you can do today!" is the cliche which makes every procrastinator cringe. Everyone has experienced putting off various duties, tasks and responsibilities until the last possible minute (or longer). Unfortunately, if this becomes a habit, it can be detrimental to the success of a business.

Procrastination tends to bring to mind words such as lazy, unproductive and inefficient, yet procrastination is not necessarily a negative state. In fact, it is simply a signal that it is time to evaluate the status of the task in question and discover the reason(s) it is staying at the bottom of the "to-do" pile.

The reasons why people procrastinate are numerous. Perhaps one of the most common is setting such high, perfectionistic expectations for performance that accomplishing the task seems overwhelming, if not impossible. It is easy to set yourself up in this manner — to never feel quite good enough, continually dissatisfied with your performance even though you got the job done. The put-off project then becomes a representation of your fears of failure and inadequacy.

Perfectionists believe that "adequate" or "sufficient" performance is not enough. "Adequate" and "inadequate" come to mean the same thing. It is important to put these three words: perfection, adequate and inadequate — in their proper perspective. Nothing is inherently wrong in having high standards but they need to be evaluated to determine if they are realistic. Perfectionism is impossible. To do a job adequately is to do what is needed. Inadequate means not meeting the requirements. If you feel fear about some task that you have to do, it could be that you are setting perfectionistic standards for yourself that are impossible to meet.

It is also useful to evaluate whether or not this task is actually necessary. If it's not something that you want to do and it's not really necessary, then maybe you can take yourself off the hook. Oftentimes people can convince themselves that a task is critical when it isn't. You must evaluate and prioritize your tasks (this may take the assistance of a consultant).

Possibly you've agreed to do a certain task or activity that you really didn't want to do. If this is the case it may not be too late to renegotiate. If you frequently find yourself having difficulty saying no and procrastinate as a result, it is time to learn how to set limits and boundaries.

Sometimes procrastination is brought on by a lack of information. If you expect yourself to do a task without having the necessary knowledge, even the most routine task can become overwhelming. Before you begin a project, map out the technical, informational and functional requirements. Once you have determined what supplies, information and other resources will be needed to complete the task — obtain them and begin your project. Being organized can make any task more palatable and run more smoothly (see Chapter Two). Additionally, give yourself permission to ask for the help you need. Asking for help can provide you with the energy and support to accomplish the task.

When procrastination simply comes down to having to do a task that must be done but is loathsome, there are some techniques to choose from that may help you move on. These techniques are reframing, task breakdown/simplification and delegation.

REFRAMING is finding an alternative way to view the project at hand. This may be done by creating a more pleasant environment to work on the task, such as listening to enjoyable music, sitting in a comfortable chair, sipping on a glass of iced tea or involving another person (preferably with a good sense of humor) in the task.

TASK BREAKDOWN involves clarifying the components and progression of a project by setting clear goals with target dates. This is basically taking things one step at a time and keeping them as simple as possible.

DELEGATION (or sub-contracting) is often an alternative. Explore the possibilities — determine if there are portions of the task (if not the whole thing) that can be done more easily and effectively by someone else. Consider trading tasks with a colleague. It is important to remember that when you delegate or trade, you are not handing over total responsibility for the finished product. You still need to oversee the tasks to assure their completion.

Procrastination is not only a personal issue, it also effects associates and staff as well. If you have discovered that you are a perfectionist, it can be extremely difficult to accurately gauge other's performance. You may be setting standards so high that not even you could attain them. Are you projecting your own perfectionism? Are you creating an atmosphere where people are afraid to take risks? Is it safe for your co-workers to make mistakes?

If this is indeed the situation, discuss it with your associates and staff. Let them know that you are aware of your tendencies and then discuss how you can improve working conditions. You need to set new standards — they can still be high, but not out of reach. If you can come to an agreement, everyone wins — you are happy, the people you work with won't feel as pressured and the company gets higher quality work from the staff.

Procrastination in self and others is an issue that most people have to deal with at some point in their lives. Procrastination is usually a symptom that something isn't right. The important thing to remember is to listen to yourself. Find out what is behind the behavior. Evaluate the dynamics. Then you will be able to alleviate the procrastination by making the necessary changes — be they internal or external.

Barriers to success need not become blockades. Strategies to overcome these barriers include: clarify your values and operate from them, do any necessary clearing work or therapy, set clear goals, become a calculated risk taker, work smarter — not harder, be informed, keep balanced, learn from your past, create a positive support system and keep things in perspective.

• TIME MANAGEMENT PRINCIPLES •

One of the keystones to self management is time management. What is time, really? Webster defines time as indefinite, unlimited duration in which things are considered as happening in the past, present or future. It is a system of measuring duration.

Time management isn't about which appointment book you use. It isn't creating a 30 hour day — everyone has the same amount of time. Time Management is about your attitudes and perceptions. It is based on realizing just how much your time is worth and choosing activities that are the highest priority for you to achieve your goals.

Time management is really a matter of how well you use your time. Time can either be an asset or a liability, it all depends on your attitudes. You can't alter time, you can only alter your attitudes and behaviors relating to time.

Your attitudes towards time are influenced by conditioning and by your level of self-esteem. What thoughts and feelings do you have concerning time? How did your family relate to time? Do you respect yourself by taking the time to take care of yourself? Do you view time as your friend or your enemy?

In terms of behavior change, many possible ways exist for taking action. Learn (or enhance) the skills that are required to improve your productivity: goal setting and strategic planning, scheduling, dealing with interruptions, being able to decline offers, delegation, being current with your job skills, product knowledge, communication skills, management skills and stress management.

Some benefits of effective time management include: being able to do the same work in less time or doing more work in the same number of hours, increasing personal productivity, getting more recognition, earning more money, decreasing frustration and stress, having more time for planning, spending more time with your family, having more time for hobbies & recreation, improving your health and experiencing increased joy and satisfaction.

The fundamental basis of time management is the Pareto (80/20) Principle: The Pareto principle states that 80% of your results are produced by 20% of your activities. And conversely, 20% of your results are produced by 80% of your activities. Time management is effective because most people spend a lot of time in activities that are not an efficient use of their time. These percentages vary for individual cases, but the principle still holds. The more you learn to focus on these 20% activities and turn them into 40% or even 60%, the more productive, prosperous and balanced you'll be.

**THERE IS A FUNDAMENTAL DIFFERENCE
BETWEEN WORKING HARDER AND WORKING SMARTER.**

• TYPES OF TIME NEEDED TO RUN A BUSINESS •

In order to effectively run your business, you must remember that there are many areas for which you need to allot time. You need time to plan, work with clients, manage the business, continue your education, promote your practice, communicate, develop ideas, take care of yourself and have fun.

Effective daily planning is crucial to time management. Many people create incredible to-do lists, but lack the motivation to complete them. When you have a clear purpose, priorities, goals and plans of action, you don't get so overwhelmed. You know what you have to do, the order in which to do it and when it needs to be done. Sometimes people imagine things to be far more complicated than they really are.

The time you spend in planning is always well invested. When you have a clear plan for the day and a crisis does occur, you are then more flexible in handling it and making any necessary adjustments. Your day flows more easily and you are more on target.

The basis of productive planning is effective goal setting. (Refer to Chapter Two for specific techniques.) The major element in planning (especially daily planning) is prioritization. After you have written your daily plan, evaluate it. Decide which activities absolutely must get done today and rate them as Imperative. Review the other items and indicate the ones that need to be done very soon by labeling them as Important. Mark the rest of the activities (the ones that it would be nice if you accomplished them, but they're not of major significance) as being Desirable. (You will find a Daily Planning Form in Appendix A. The form is provided as an example for you to adapt to your specific needs.)

When you first do planning it may seem to take a long time, but after you do it on a regular basis, you will be able to plan your day very quickly. Remember, planning is to ultimately simplify your life — not make it more complicated.

MANAGING YOUR BUSINESS is covered from both a philosophical viewpoint and a business skills perspective in Chapters Three and Four. We often forget to schedule appropriate time for the day-to-day tasks such as doing laundry, making phone calls, supervising staff (if you have any), keeping files and purchasing supplies. All of these activities take time, sometimes a lot more time than anticipated.

Another aspect of managing your business has to do with respecting yourself and time in relation to bartering (or trading) services. Bartering is a wonderful method for obtaining products and services for which you prefer to not purchase with cash. Unfortunately, some people get so into bartering that they never earn any money. Be very clear of your reasons for trading. Before you do any type of bartering, ask yourself if you would spend money on that product or service if you had the cash. If not, don't trade. Also, remember that barter is considered taxable income by the Internal Revenue Service.

WORKING WITH CLIENTS is the area where most of your time is spent. Your ability to effectively schedule your appointments greatly impacts your success and your stress level. It is important to have sufficient time between clients and yet not leave large blocks of unproductive time. You may discover that you need to schedule an extra half hour for new clients. Other clients may need more time. You may need a longer recuperation time after certain clients. The longer you are in practice, the more adept you become in judging how much time is necessary to spend with clients and between sessions.

CONTINUING YOUR EDUCATION is necessary to your career. It is important to always be broadening your knowledge, particularly in the areas of interpersonal skills, product knowledge, technical skills and business skills. Some ways to do that are: reading magazines and books, taking classes, attending seminars, watching videos and networking. Benjamin Franklin said, "If you fill your mind with coins from your purse, your mind will fill your purse with coins."

DEVELOPING IDEAS is one of the most exciting and creative aspects of any business. Always be open to new opportunities. Brainstorm ways to streamline your procedures. Find methods to reduce your effort by diversifying your practice (e.g., hire employees, sell products and subcontract out work to other practitioners and take a percentage of the fees). Create ways in which you are able to work in essence with more than one client at a time (e.g., offer group sessions, give seminars and publish articles and books). The possibilities are abundant!

PROMOTING YOUR PRACTICE is vital to your success. This is the aspect of business that most healing arts practitioners overlook. You can't rely on your clients to bring you more new clients (see Chapter Five). Promotion is necessary during all phases of your business. When you first start your practice, you may spend more hours promoting than actually working with clients. Then, even when your business seems to be established, you still need to actively promote yourself. People move, change practitioners, try alternate methods of self-improvement, etc. I have known several very successful healing arts practitioners whose businesses appeared to fall apart over night. They were not promoting themselves very well; they hadn't noticed the changes that were occurring until it was too late. So, they had to "start all over again". You can avoid this through regular promotion. It is critical that you invest at least fifteen percent of your work time in promotion.

COMMUNICATING is essential to your business. You need to be able to fully understand your clients and their needs. You spend most of your communication time in listening, and yet most people have never been taught how to listen. When talking with your clients, focus on the message — not the method of delivery. Delay making any evaluations. Take responsibility for understanding what you are hearing. If you are not certain you understand what you have heard, ask questions or rephrase what you think you heard.

HAVING FUN tends to be one of the least planned aspects of life. People are inclined to leave their enjoyment to chance. Remember to balance your professional goals with your personal goals. Be sure to include fun in your life EVERY DAY!

TAKING CARE OF YOURSELF is imperative, but unfortunately most people put themselves last. It is so easy to get caught up in your business and being there for others, that literally no time is left for you. It is important to take care of yourself mentally, physically, emotionally and spiritually. Make sure that every day you do at least one thing just for yourself. Respect your needs and wants. Create a support system for your business and personal life. Care-givers have a tendency to not allow themselves to be care-receivers. Don't let yourself fall into that syndrome. Allot however much time is needed to take care of **you**.

One of the major factors that influences your time is stress. If you do not handle stress productively, you can waste hours of time each day — not to mention time lost due to stress-related illness. Make certain that you exercise regularly and follow a healthy eating plan.

Take a five minute break every two hours to stretch your muscles, do some deep breathing, exercise your eyes and revitalize yourself.

Keeping balance in mind is the key to stress management. You need to keep things in perspective. Don't react to things that aren't your responsibility. Learn to deal with interruptions: internal and external. Learn how to say no.

Last, but most definitely not least, it's crucial that you develop and maintain a positive self-image. You must be true to yourself. Make certain that your needs and wants are being met. Live your life (and run your business) according to your values and principles.

It is important to recognize that there are different types of time you need and the amount of time spent in each category may vary from day to day. It is imperative to set a regular schedule for your business. Decide what days and what hours you will work. You may want to do this on a weekly or monthly basis. Once you've made your schedule, stick to it. Even if you don't have the time slots filled with clients, you can always do other business activities. It can be so tempting to look at your appointment book, not see anything scheduled for the afternoon, and decide to go play. Occasionally this is fine, but be careful it doesn't become a habit.

On the following page is an exercise to assist you in clarifying your high priority activities. You may be surprised at what you discover. The objective of this is exercise is for you to take this list and begin concentrating your time and energy on items you've rated as being the most crucial to your success.

TIME CAN BE YOUR ENEMY OR YOUR FRIEND.
IT BECOMES YOUR FRIEND WHEN YOU LEARN HOW TO MANAGE YOURSELF.

• HIGH PRIORITY ACTIVITIES •

High priority activities are the "20%" ones that produce 80% of your results. Before you can begin to increase the time spent in those important activities, you must identify them.

Think about the various activities involved in your business. List at least ten of the most important things you do in the center column on the form below. Then in the left hand column rate them in the order you think is most important to your success. In the right hand column rate them in the order of how much time you spend in each activity.

IMPORTANCE	ACTIVITY	TIME SPENT
_____	_____	_____
_____	_____	_____
_____	_____	_____
_____	_____	_____
_____	_____	_____
_____	_____	_____
_____	_____	_____
_____	_____	_____
_____	_____	_____
_____	_____	_____
_____	_____	_____
_____	_____	_____
_____	_____	_____

The more you focus on your high priority activities, the more productive you will be. You may also discover some conflicts. If this happens, refer to your purpose, priorities and goals. They usually will provide direction. Sometimes you have to make difficult decisions and then either delegate the other activities, simplify them or eliminate them. It is also recommended that you show your list to a colleague. It is possible that you overlooked something or you may need to switch some of your priorities — and it's usually easier for someone else to be objective.

• TRACKING •

Frequently, in business, we have no idea why things are going the way they are — even when they are going well. Was it that last ad? Could it have been that interview in the newspaper? Maybe it was the new brochure? Or was it due to extending office hours on Thursday? Even though it's not always possible to know for certain the exact action that generated (or didn't) the desired results, you greatly increase your knowledge and optimize your efforts by tracking the important components.

Tracking is a documentation of your progress used to illustrate trends. Frequently your appointment book and checkbook don't really tell you the whole truth. A lot of critical data is not included in those books and if you use them as your major reference point for judging your success, you may find yourself in a predicament. Oftentimes things are not as they appear.

For example, imagine that you have been fairly well booked and have had a satisfactory level of income for the last few months, so you haven't been putting much attention into marketing. Then the next month goes by and you discover (to your dismay) that your client load has decreased and your income level has significantly dropped. You don't quite understand how this could happen — after all, everything seemed to be going so well. You decide to carefully review your books and find that you've only had three new clients in the last two months, four clients have completed their work with you and the time between sessions for the rest of your clients has been substantially increasing. Had you been keeping track of that kind of information on a summary sheet or a graph, you could have noticed the trend earlier and taken action sooner (e.g., done some type of marketing) to rebuild your clientele base. In any business, particularly one that's small, one slow month can be devastating.

Tracking can help you anticipate potential problems so that you can take the appropriate steps to avoid or overcome the obstacles and modify the direction of the trend more to your liking. Tracking is dynamic in nature, it focuses on the way things change — the "motion" of business.

Another example of how tracking can be helpful has to do with timing. You may notice that for the last three years, your business drops dramatically every October. Using that information you can decide to increase your advertising and promotion in August and September or you may just choose to take advantage of the slow period and plan your vacation for October. Conversely, it wouldn't be judicious for you to plan a vacation during your peak period.

TRACKING TOOLS —

The methods for tracking are varied. You might use graph paper, spread sheets, custom designed forms or simple notebook paper. Make the forms very clear and as straightforward as possible to fill out. Also, be certain to design your client forms so they provide you with information (e.g., how they heard about you), demographics and session notes for your tracking sheets. You may want to make charts and post them on the wall or put your tracking forms into a notebook.

Experiment with tracking activities on a daily, weekly, monthly or quarterly basis. Consistency is essential in tracking, particularly when tracking the results of marketing campaigns, since it often takes several months to discern those results. Additionally, you may discover that the results were due to a combination of factors. Thus the measurable benefits of tracking derive from the knowledge you receive over the long-run.

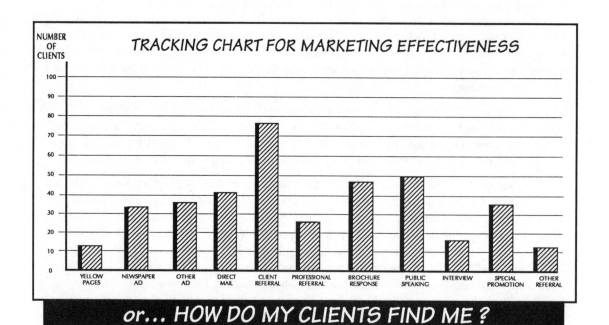

or... HOW DO MY CLIENTS FIND ME ?

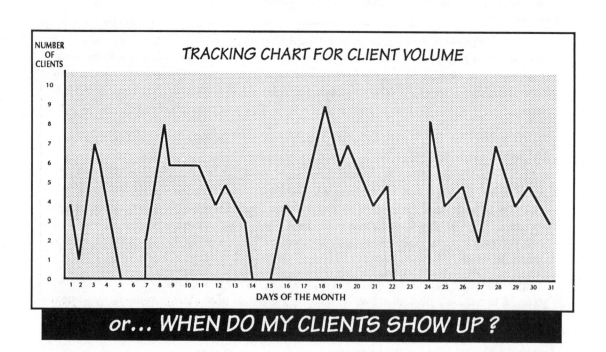

or... WHEN DO MY CLIENTS SHOW UP ?

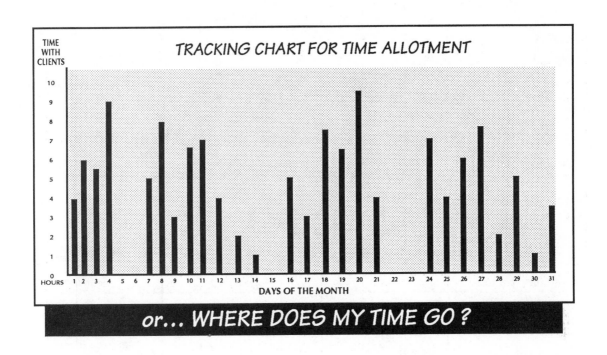

or... WHERE DOES MY TIME GO ?

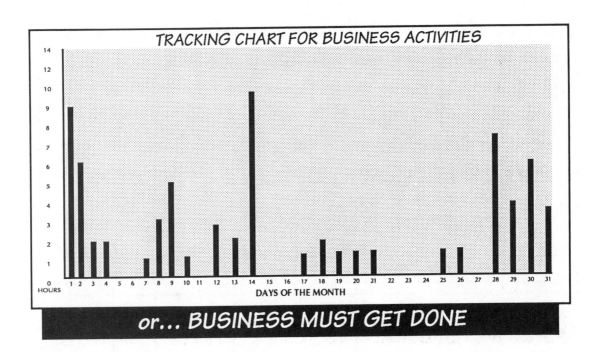

or... BUSINESS MUST GET DONE

Time Tracking Sheet —

	Mon	Tue	Wed	Thu	Fri	Sat	Sun	Goal	Actual
health	20 min 10		30	20	60	10		3 hr	2.5
exercise	30	30		30	30	60		3	3
reading	10	20	60		30		120	3	4
planning	30	10	20	5	10		15	2	1.5
phone	90	30	30 30	10 15	5			2	3.5
appointments	90 140	60 70		80 130	90	80 160		14	15
driving	30 60		20	60	40	30 30		5	4.5
promo/networking	90	60 60	90	30	30 60			5	7
seminars								0	0
bookkeeping	10	20	10 30	10			40	1	2
proposals		30						1	.5
client files	10 5	5		10 10	20 5	10	15	1	1.5
repair/maintenance	10 10	30	10	20	10 10		20	1	2
letters				60			120	1	3
follow-up	20	25	35	20	20			1	2
operations	15		15		20	10		1	1
meetings		30		60				1	1.5
volunteer			180						
play	40	60	70	40	140	310	120	14	13
TOTAL	**12**	**9**	**10.5**	**10**	**9.5**	**12**	**7.5**	**62**	**70.5**

Useful Items To Track —

- Client demographics

- Total number of clients

- Types of clients

- Session time spent per client

- Time spent per client in adjunct support

- Time between sessions

- Type of techniques utilized

- Number of sessions per client

- Average cost of total treatment plan

- How your clients heard about you

- Referrals generated by specific marketing campaigns

- Time spent in all business activities

- Total Income (daily, weekly, monthly, etc.)

- Total Expenses

This data provides you with the information you need to assess the progress of your long term goals and strategies, as well as enhancing your decision-making abilities when it comes to planning your future marketing campaigns and general business direction.

Tracking is an essential component in making a business plan work. First you must decide what you want to track. The above list, your business plan and your list of high priority activities are excellent places to begin.

Studies have shown that tracking in itself increases your productivity. It is an excellent way to keep yourself motivated, evaluate your status and help you determine the most appropriate areas in which to invest your time and money in order to build your practice.

As with daily planning, it usually takes a little while to become adept at the skill of tracking. After you have experimented with various forms, you will discover the ones that are most appropriate for your needs and then it won't take you very much time at all to track.

Invest the time required for tracking — it's an informational and inspirational tool to help you run a productive and profitable business.

• THE ART OF RISK-TAKING •

Two commonly heard cliches are "nothing ventured, nothing gained" and "no guts, no glory". Taking risks is an integral part of business — it's the doorway to success, yet the art is in knowing how to take smart risks. You are placing yourself in a potentially ongoing risky environment just by being in the healing arts profession since this field is still not fully sanctioned by the general public. Some people consider themselves to be risk-takers when in reality they are simply daredevils. Taking risks is not about blindly jumping into any situation. It is essential that you understand the components of risk-taking, learn how to minimize your potential losses and strengthen your risk-taking abilities.

The two major elements that influence your capability to successfully manage risks are the level of comfort you have in experiencing new or unusual situations and your self-esteem. Think about the source of your self-confidence. To what degree do you base it upon your opinions and values? How much do you look to others for validation? Is your behavior mainly motivated by external factors such as social approval and material consequences or by internal considerations such as your beliefs and feelings? In terms of self-esteem, the primary discomfort in taking risks stems from the fear of rejection. In considering your ability to feel confident in novel circumstances, the fundamental discomfort is usually due to inexperience. People tend to take the safer routes so often that they haven't developed a bank of experiences on which to draw. Reflect upon your childhood. What messages were you given regarding the safety of your environment? How did your family deal with crises? What behaviors did you learn to adopt? You can alleviate a lot of anxiety by keeping your expectations realistic and embracing the opportunities for new experiences.

Risk-takers are achievers. They are not content with maintaining the status quo. They prefer action to inaction and tend to follow through on their goals with little hesitation. They are exhilarated by challenges rather than intimidated by them and proceed despite their fears. They carefully evaluate risks and develop strategic plans of action. They can distinguish the facts from their emotions, which enables them to handle crises well and empowers them. Risk-takers have a strong commitment to being the best they can be.

THE DO'S OF RISK-TAKING —

- Do have a life plan with clear goals.

- Do make sure the risk is aligned with your life plan.

- Do evaluate the potential gains and losses.

- Do ask questions and research the situation.

- Do know your strengths and limitations.

- Do brainstorm several alternatives.

- Do list potential conflicts and solutions.

- Do set a realistic timetable.

- Do be flexible.

- Do trust your intuition and instincts.

- Do follow through and give it your best.

- Do review and possibly revise your strategy.

- Do ask for support.

- Do acknowledge the people who give you support.

The Don'ts of Risk-Taking —

- Don't be unrealistic.

- Don't be a perfectionist.

- Don't deny your feelings.

- Don't ignore or minimize problems.

- Don't mistake emotions for facts.

- Don't rush.

- Don't procrastinate.

- Don't blame others for your mistakes.

- Don't give up too soon.

- Don't be afraid to cut your losses and move on.

- Don't trust blindly.

- Don't risk just to prove yourself to others.

- Don't combine too many risks at once.

Developing your adeptness in taking risks is a lifelong process. As you go through life, the stakes just seem to get higher. Build your repertoire of risk-taking experiences. This assists you in being able to successfully manage risks. By drawing upon your past experiences to see the similarities to the current condition, you are better able to determine an effective solution. Put yourself in situations that require you to exercise your creative problem solving abilities. Start with low-risk situations and gradually increase your confidence level so that you feel more comfortable even when the risks are great.

The continual enhancement of your self image is vital in cultivating risk-taking behaviors. Begin with positive self-talk. Fill your mind with thoughts about your potential. Become grounded in the knowledge that you are your own source of power and that this power is an honorable trait. Expect to succeed. Release some of your conditioned apprehension and fear by doing clearing exercises such as the following: Think about a situation that makes you feel uneasy. Imagine what is the very worst thing that could possibly happen. Then evaluate the situation. Is it really that bad? Are your fears justified? Finally, visualize yourself being comfortable and confident while in that risky situation.

Your attitudes about the world can greatly influence your facility in taking risks. Be enthusiastic about the present and future. Expand your view of life. Focus on the prospects for success and joy. Don't become immersed in the potentials for disaster. Accurately evaluate what would really happen if you were to take a risk and not succeed. Remember that success lies in taking action.

The last factor that tends to really impact people's freedom to take chances are finances. Most people are overly concerned with money. The truth is that most successful entrepreneurs have gone bankrupt at least once before finally making it. Again, you are the best judge of what's appropriate. You are the only one who can determine whether or not a risk is worth taking. One step you can take right now is to reduce your debt as much as possible. If you are considering taking a risk that has financial ramifications, take the time to thoroughly evaluate the possibilities. Often what is more scary than the possibility of losing money is the potential for losing face.

Life is filled with risks. You can increase your comfort level and capabilities to successfully manage risks by purposefully putting yourself in gradually increasing risky situations. Invest the required time and energy to accurately evaluate and strategically plan your risks. Keep in mind that everyone makes mistakes. After all, if there wasn't a chance for failure, things wouldn't be risky.

• CHOOSING ADVISORS •

Every business has management, legal and accounting aspects. It is important to know people you trust to advise you, particularly in the areas where you lack knowledge, interest or skill. Selecting the most appropriate advisors will have a direct effect on the success of your business. Before you make any major decisions, discuss them with at least one other person — regardless of your expertise in the area. All too often the tendency is to want to do it all on your own, and it's almost impossible to be truly objective, especially with something as significant as your business/career. Your primary advisors are your lawyer, accountant and banker, followed by your business consultant.

Pick the members of your advisory team before you actually NEED them. Don't wait for an emergency. You may not have ample time to find an appropriate advisor and deal with the situation at hand. Begin to build your relationships now (particularly with a banker) so you can establish your credibility and develop rapport.

The process for selecting trustworthy advisors begins by getting personal recommendations from friends and colleagues. In addition to the names, get specific information about them. Find out why they recommend these people and what types of dealings have they had with them. Whatever you do, don't stop at this point. You must also make your own assessments. The first thing is to trust your intuition. If you don't feel comfortable with someone — keep looking. Even if you feel good about the person, do further research. S/he may be an excellent advisor but not appropriate for you.

Check into the potential advisor's credentials and competency. If s/he has the required expertise and experience, the next phase is to discover if you are compatible. Find out the type of clientele s/he tends to work with. Has s/he had many clients in your profession?

Next see if your personalities and styles mesh. Take into consideration that if this is someone you are going to work with for a long time, it's important that you share a similar philosophy and manner in which you like to get things done.

The subsequent step is to assess your level of confidence and trust in this person — professionally and personally. One of the most critical factors in choosing an advisor is in how well you are able to communicate with each other. This person may be totally qualified, works with many others in your profession, has an impeccable character, shares many of the same beliefs as you, etc., but it seems as though whenever you talk, you are speaking in two different languages. You have to decide whether or not it's worth the time (and money) it takes to work through the communication barriers in order to have this person be an advisor.

Finally, you have to determine if this person desires to have you as a client. Does s/he demonstrate a sense of commitment to you and your business? Is s/he available to answer questions when you need them? Finding appropriate advisors is not always an easy task, but it can mean the difference between business difficulties (or even failure) and success.

• MOTIVATION •

Motivation is about satisfying desires and needs. Abraham Maslow's hierarchy of needs are physiological (satisfaction of hunger, thirst and sex), safety (security and stability), social (belongingness and love), esteem (self-respect and ego) and self-actualization. It is extraordinarily difficult to be motivated towards self-actualization if your safety or ego needs aren't being met.

So if you find that you just can't motivate yourself to do a particular task, find out what other needs you have that are not being met. You must appeal to the needs and desires that are the strongest at any given moment. Once you have satisfied those other needs, it is easier to complete the specific task.

The two most common types of motivation are fear and incentive motivation, both of which have serious shortcomings. Fear motivation is one of the oldest, easiest and universally least effective means of motivation. It forces you to act out of fear of the consequences. Parents frequently use this technique with young children. The primary limitation of this style of motivation is that most people (particularly children) can quickly build up a tolerance to fear, and since the repercussions are rarely enforced, they usually aren't taken seriously.

Incentive motivation promises a reward for behavior. This method is often used in business as a way to increase productivity. It is also frequently used by people in the process of altering habits. The problems associated with this motivation system are that the rewards have to keep getting bigger as time goes by in order to have the same impact, and withholding the reward represents a punishment. Incentive motivation won't satisfy your desire for achievement.

The most effective motivation is self-motivation, being inspired by the sheer joy of accomplishment. Approaching life from this point of view is extremely empowering to yourself and those around you. It can be very freeing when you don't need outside stimulus to induce action. Sometimes this can be difficult because quite often the results of your actions are intangible or may not be realized for a long time. Self-motivation is an attitude that takes time to develop and fully integrate into your life. It may take you a longer time to master your motivation in some areas of your life than in others.

Your history plays a major role in your attitude development. Throughout your life you have been influenced to some degree by your environment and the other people in your life. Your cumulative experiences and feelings impact your perception. For example, you may view a certain task as boring while someone else might find the same task exciting. One technique for altering your feelings about an activity (and thus making it easier to accomplish) is to remove any negative descriptive terms associated with it. The key factor in motivation is goals. Without goals, there is nothing toward which to be motivated. You may even want to create goals about motivation. Your mind is a powerful tool that is ready and waiting for you to utilize more effectively. Left unused, the mind finds ways to amuse itself, not always to your advantage.

In any career, you experience ups and downs. The key is to recognize the difference between a natural phase and downward spiral. Step back and objectively (as possible) evaluate the situation. Determine what is really happening. Ask yourself the following questions: What goals aren't being met? Why? What can be done about them? Is it too late? How can this situation be avoided in the future? After you have assessed the situation and brainstormed ideas for managing the predicament, discuss the issue with an advisor. Get some feedback from a different perspective.

If you are still not able to motivate yourself, do some clearing exercises as described in Chapter One. Oftentimes, people lack inspiration and determination because of negative thought patterns and conditioning. Sentence completion exercises are an excellent method for releasing energy associated with negative conditioning. If you are having difficulties with a specific problem, first take an honest look to see if you are truly willing to resolve the problem. If you are, put aside approximately two hours and do the following clearing exercise.

DISSOLVING PROBLEMS —

Take some notebook paper and write the following questions on the top of each sheet of paper, putting one question per piece of paper and keeping them in the order given. Spend at least five minutes per page actually doing the exercise. (Please refer to Chapter One for detailed instructions on Sentence Completions.)

- What is the area you are having difficulty with? Describe in detail.

- What are your fears and attitudes regarding your problem?

- What aren't you getting?

- What are you getting that you don't want?

- What are you getting that you do want?

- In regards to this problem, how have you been trying to resolve it?

- In regards to this problem, what do you think you should be doing?

- What is it that you want?

- What is it that you think you should want?

- What are the benefits of not resolving this problem?

- What would you have to give up in order to resolve this problem?

- What would you have to realize in order to resolve this problem?

- What are you holding onto or protecting in regards to your problem?

- Who or what is limiting you?

- By solving this problem, what new problems will be created?

- What is it that you really want?

- What are the specific things you will do to resolve this problem?

You are the only one who can motivate yourself. Developing a healthy attitude towards yourself is the cornerstone to self-motivation. Sometimes people don't feel motivated to accomplish certain goals because they really don't care about the goals in the first place. Be honest with yourself. If you really don't want to do something, don't try to convince yourself that you do want to achieve it.

The clearer you are about your purposes, priorities and goals, the easier and more natural it will be to become motivated by the sheer act of attaining your goals. Therein lies true motivation.

• SELF ASSESSMENT •

You already have been doing a lot of soul-searching and clearing throughout the process of "working" this book. Now it's time to evaluate yourself in order to determine the skills you need to learn and/or enhance. Be honest.

What are your strengths?

_____

_____

_____

_____

_____

What are your limitations?

_____

_____

_____

_____

_____

How do you intend to alleviate those limitations?

_____

_____

_____

_____

_____

The key to being successful in the business world while staying balanced lies in self management. Invest the time required to enhance these skills. Improve your time management abilities, create plans of action, set realistic goals, clarify your values, take educational courses, learn new skills, take care of yourself, stay balanced and most important of all — acknowledge your progress and celebrate your successes!

The following chart is a summation of the principles and techniques covered in this book. Refer to it often.

I WISH YOU GREAT JOY AND PROSPERITY IN ALL YOU DO!

• BE YOUR OWN BEST MANAGER •

Identify your values and operate from them

Clarify your purpose, priorities & goals

Design and implement an effective business plan

Create strategic plans of action

Learn to work smarter — not harder

Track important components

Eliminate time wasters

Plan your days

Set a schedule & keep it

Be dressed for "work"

Get feedback from colleagues and experts

Collect information: quotes, articles, statistics

Keep your work space organized

Enhance your telephone skills

Follow through with clients

Market your business consistently

Join at least one professional association

Develop powerful networking abilities

Keep accurate records

Be a calculated risk-taker

Be willing to move on

Make sure your needs are being met

Exercise regularly

Create a support system

Continue your education

Get out of the house/office EVERY DAY!!!

Remember, we're all human — we make mistakes

Keep things in perspective

Take responsibility for yourself

Choose appropriate advisors

If there are tasks you hate — delegate (or subcontract)

Respect you mind's and/or body's cycles

Balance your personal & professional life

Acknowledge your accomplishments every day

APPENDIX A

• WHEEL OF LIFE •

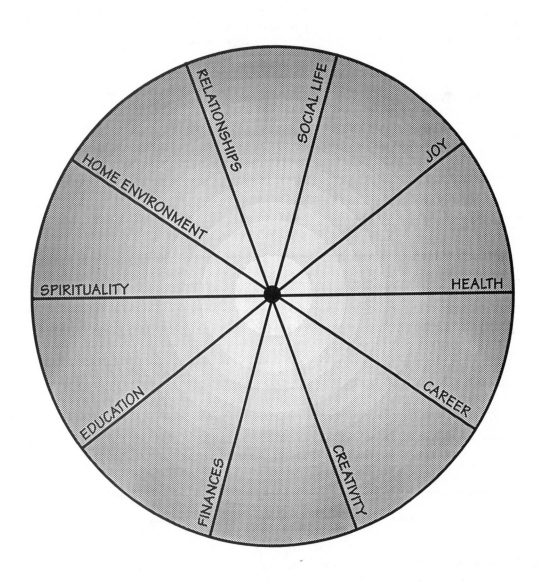

• HIGH PRIORITY ACTIVITIES •

High priority activities are the "20%" ones that produce 80% of your results. Before you can begin to increase the time spent in those important activities, you must identify them.

Think about the various activities involved in your business. List at least ten of the most important things you do in the center column on the form below. Then in the left hand column rate them in the order you think is most important to your success. In the right hand column rate them in the order of how much time you spend in each activity.

IMPORTANCE	ACTIVITY	TIME SPENT
_____	_____	_____
_____	_____	_____
_____	_____	_____
_____	_____	_____
_____	_____	_____
_____	_____	_____
_____	_____	_____
_____	_____	_____
_____	_____	_____
_____	_____	_____
_____	_____	_____
_____	_____	_____
_____	_____	_____
_____	_____	_____
_____	_____	_____
_____	_____	_____

The more you focus on your high priority activities, the more productive you will be. You may also discover some conflicts. If this happens, refer to your purpose, priorities and goals. They usually will provide direction. Sometimes you have to make difficult decisions and then either delegate the other activities, simplify them or eliminate them. It is also recommended that you show your list to a colleague. It is possible that you overlooked something or you may need to switch some of your priorities — and it's usually easier for someone else to be objective.

• DAILY PLAN •

Day/Date: _____

Purpose: _____

Priorities: _____

_____

_____

_____

Goals: _____

_____

_____

_____

Thought for the Day: _____

What supplies/Information do I need? _____

_____

_____

— TO DO LIST —

IMPERATIVE: **IMPORTANT:**

_____   _____

_____   _____

_____   _____

_____   _____

_____   _____

_____   **DESIRABLE:**

_____   _____

_____   _____

_____   _____

_____   _____

What did I accomplish today? _____

_____

• TIME TRACKING SHEET •

	Mon	Tue	Wed	Thu	Fri	Sat	Sun	Goal	Actual
health									
exercise									
reading									
planning									
phone									
appointments									
driving									
promo/networking									
seminars									
bookkeeping									
proposals									
client files									
repair/maintenance									
letters									
follow-up									
operations									
meetings									
volunteer									
play									
TOTAL									

• STRATEGIC PLANNING •

TODAY'S DATE: _____ TARGET DATE: _____ DATE ACHIEVED:_____

PURPOSE: _____

_____

PRIORITY: _____

_____

SITUATION DESCRIPTION: _____

_____

_____

OBJECTIVE: _____
❑ Capitalize on this strength   ❑ Change this condition   ❑ Other

GOAL: _____

_____

BENEFITS OF ACHIEVING THIS GOAL: _____

_____

_____

_____

POSSIBLE COURSES OF ACTION:

1. _____

_____

2. _____

_____

3. _____

_____

4. _____

_____

BEST COURSE: _____

_____

_____

_____

PROPOSALS/OUTLINE:

1. _____

   _____

2. _____

   _____

3. _____

   _____

4. _____

   _____

ADVANTAGES: _____

_____

_____

_____

_____

POTENTIAL CONFLICTS/DISADVANTAGES:	SOLUTIONS:
1. _____	1. _____
2. _____	2. _____
3. _____	3. _____
4. _____	4. _____
5. _____	5. _____
6. _____	6. _____

ACTION REQUIRED TO BEGIN: _____

_____

_____

_____

RESOURCES NEEDED: _____

_____

_____

_____

SPECIFIC STEPS TO ACHIEVE THIS GOAL	TARGET DATE	PERSON RESPONSIBLE
1. _____	_____	_____
2. _____	_____	_____
3. _____	_____	_____
4. _____	_____	_____
5. _____	_____	_____
6. _____	_____	_____
7. _____	_____	_____
8. _____	_____	_____
9. _____	_____	_____
10. _____	_____	_____
11. _____	_____	_____
12. _____	_____	_____
13. _____	_____	_____
14. _____	_____	_____
15. _____	_____	_____
16. _____	_____	_____
17. _____	_____	_____
18. _____	_____	_____
19. _____	_____	_____
20. _____	_____	_____
21. _____	_____	_____
22. _____	_____	_____
23. _____	_____	_____
24. _____	_____	_____
25. _____	_____	_____

• CONTACT/REFERRAL RECORDS •

Name _____

Company _____

Title _____

Address _____

Phone (w) _____ **(h)** _____

Referred By: _____

Follow-up: _____

_____

Notes _____

_____

_____

_____

Date	Time	Action/Outcome

• CLIENT DESCRIPTION TRACKING FORM •

Name	Date of First Session	Date of Last Session	Total Number of Sessions	Average Fee Collected	How Client Found You
_____	_____	_____	_____	_____	_____
_____	_____	_____	_____	_____	_____
_____	_____	_____	_____	_____	_____
_____	_____	_____	_____	_____	_____
_____	_____	_____	_____	_____	_____
_____	_____	_____	_____	_____	_____
_____	_____	_____	_____	_____	_____
_____	_____	_____	_____	_____	_____
_____	_____	_____	_____	_____	_____
_____	_____	_____	_____	_____	_____
_____	_____	_____	_____	_____	_____
_____	_____	_____	_____	_____	_____
_____	_____	_____	_____	_____	_____
_____	_____	_____	_____	_____	_____
_____	_____	_____	_____	_____	_____
_____	_____	_____	_____	_____	_____
_____	_____	_____	_____	_____	_____
_____	_____	_____	_____	_____	_____
_____	_____	_____	_____	_____	_____
_____	_____	_____	_____	_____	_____

Total number of clients: _____ Average time span: _____

Average number of sessions: _____ Total average fee: _____

Most frequent ways clients learned about you: _____

_____

_____

• CLIENT RECORDS •

Client Name _____

Address _____

Phone (w) _____ (h) _____

Referred By: _____

Date	Services	Session Length	Charges	Credits	Balance	Comments

New clients referred by above client:			
Name	Date of First Session	Cumulative # of Sessions	Cumulative Fees Collected

• CLIENT FILE INTAKE FORM •

Name: _____ Sex: M _____ F_____

Address: _____

City: _____ State: _____ Zip: _____

Telephone #: (____)_____ Social Security #: _____

Date of Birth: _____ Driver's License #: _____

Occupation: _____ Employer: _____

Employer's Address: _____

Marital Status: Single _____ Married _____Widow(er)_____Divorced _____

Number of Children: _____ Ages: _____

Name of Spouse/Significant Other: _____

Occupation: _____ Employer:_____

Insurance Carrier: _____ Policy #: _____ ID #: _____

Address: _____

City: _____ State: _____ Zip: _____

Telephone #: (____)_____

Family Physician:_____

Address: _____

City: _____ State: _____ Zip: _____

Telephone #: (____)_____

In Case of Emergency, Please Notify:

Telephone #: (____)_____ Name: _____

*Please note that if you are billing insurance companies, your clients will have to
fill out a claim form (most likely a HCFA-1500) that will duplicate most of this information.

• CLIENT FILE HEALTH INFORMATION SHEET •

Client: _____ Date: _____

Who referred you to this office? _____

Have you ever seen a [your profession here] before? _____

What are your intentions and/or expectations for this visit? _____

_____

_____

Are you now under medical/therapeutic treatment? _____

If so, for what condition? _____

Please list your doctor's name and phone number: _____

_____

List any medications you are taking (including aspirin): _____

_____

Please list (date and description) any accidents or operations: _____

_____

_____

Please circle any of the symptoms or physical problems listed below that you are currently experiencing or have experienced.

Allergies	Diabetes	Epilepsy
Arthritis	Scoliosis	Headaches
Respiratory/Lungs	Speech	Dizziness
Weakness	Indigestion	Sciatic
Hearing	High/Low Blood Pressure	Insomnia
Cardiovascular/Heart	Vision/Contacts	Fatigue
Numbness	Poor Memory	Other

• CLIENT FILE TREATMENT PLAN •

CLIENT: _____ DATE: _____

ASSESSMENT: _____

_____

_____

_____

GOALS: _____

_____

_____

_____

CLIENT PREFERENCES: _____

_____

_____

_____

TREATMENT PLAN: _____

_____

_____

_____

NOTES: _____

_____

_____

_____

• CLIENT FILE SESSION NOTES •

CLIENT: _____ DATE: _____

CURRENT SESSION NUMBER: _____ DATE OF FIRST SESSION: _____

OBSERVATIONS: _____

_____

_____

GOALS FOR THIS SESSION: _____

_____

_____

DESCRIPTION OF SPECIFIC TECHNIQUES USED: _____

_____

_____

WERE THE GOALS ACHIEVED? _____

_____

_____

GOALS AND NOTES FOR FURTHER SESSIONS: _____

_____

_____

OTHER RECOMMENDATIONS TO CLIENT: _____

_____

_____

COMMENTS: _____

_____

_____

_____

_____

• BUSINESS MILEAGE SHEET •

DATE	BEGINNING MILEAGE	ENDING MILEAGE	TOTAL MILEAGE	DESTINATION	PURPOSE
____	____	____	____	____	____
____	____	____	____	____	____
____	____	____	____	____	____
____	____	____	____	____	____
____	____	____	____	____	____
____	____	____	____	____	____
____	____	____	____	____	____
____	____	____	____	____	____
____	____	____	____	____	____
____	____	____	____	____	____
____	____	____	____	____	____
____	____	____	____	____	____
____	____	____	____	____	____
____	____	____	____	____	____
____	____	____	____	____	____
____	____	____	____	____	____
____	____	____	____	____	____
____	____	____	____	____	____
____	____	____	____	____	____
____	____	____	____	____	____
____	____	____	____	____	____
____	____	____	____	____	____
____	____	____	____	____	____
____	____	____	____	____	____

• BANK RECONCILIATION FORM •

Balance   /   /19____   _____

Plus Receipts   _____

Less Disbursements   _____

Balance   /   /19____   _____

Balance Statement   /   /19____   _____

Deposits In Transit   _____

                                 _____

                                 _____

                                 _____

Plus Total Deposits In Transit   _____

Outstanding Checks   _____

                                 _____

                                 _____

                                 _____

                                 _____

                                 _____

                                 _____

                                 _____

                                 _____

                                 _____

                                 _____

                                 _____

Less Total Outstanding Checks   _____

Bank Balance   /   /19____   _____

• MONTHLY BUSINESS EXPENSE WORKSHEET •

EXPENSE	ESTIMATED MONTHLY COST	x 12
Rent	$ _____	$ _____
Utilities	$ _____	$ _____
Telephone	$ _____	$ _____
Bank fees	$ _____	$ _____
Supplies	$ _____	$ _____
Stationery & Business Cards	$ _____	$ _____
Networking club dues	$ _____	$ _____
Education (seminars, books, professional journals, etc.)	$ _____	$ _____
Business Car (payments, gas, repairs, etc.)	$ _____	$ _____
Advertising & Promotion	$ _____	$ _____
Postage	$ _____	$ _____
Entertainment	$ _____	$ _____
Repair, Cleaning & Maintenance	$ _____	$ _____
Travel	$ _____	$ _____
Business Loan Payments	$ _____	$ _____
Salary/Draw*	$ _____	$ _____
Staff Salaries	$ _____	$ _____
Miscellaneous Insurance	$ _____	$ _____
Taxes	$ _____	$ _____
Professional Fees	$ _____	$ _____
Decorations	$ _____	$ _____
Furniture & Fixtures	$ _____	$ _____
Equipment	$ _____	$ _____
Inventory	$ _____	$ _____
Other	$ _____	$ _____

TOTAL MONTHLY $ _____

TOTAL YEARLY $ _____

In most instances it is not wise or appropriate to take draw for the first 6-12 months.

• MONTHLY PERSONAL BUDGET EXPENSE WORKSHEET •

	ESTIMATED MONTHLY COST	x 12
INCOME		
Income (draw) from business	$ _____	$ _____
Income from other sources	$ _____	$ _____
TOTAL INCOME	**$ _____**	**$ _____**
EXPENSES		
Rent	$ _____	$ _____
Home Insurance	$ _____	$ _____
Health Insurance	$ _____	$ _____
Utilities	$ _____	$ _____
Telephone	$ _____	$ _____
Auto:		
payments	$ _____	$ _____
gas	$ _____	$ _____
maintenance	$ _____	$ _____
insurance	$ _____	$ _____
other	$ _____	$ _____
Food	$ _____	$ _____
Household Supplies	$ _____	$ _____
Clothing	$ _____	$ _____
Laundry/Dry Cleaning	$ _____	$ _____
Education	$ _____	$ _____
Entertainment	$ _____	$ _____
Travel	$ _____	$ _____
Contributions	$ _____	$ _____
Health	$ _____	$ _____
Home Repair and Maintenance	$ _____	$ _____
Self Development	$ _____	$ _____
Outstanding Loans and Credit Card Payments	$ _____	$ _____
Miscellaneous Expenses	$ _____	$ _____
TOTAL EXPENSES	**$ _____**	**$ _____**
BALANCE (+/-)	**$ _____**	**$ _____**

APPENDIX B

• BUSINESS RESOURCE ORGANIZATIONS •

This directory lists general national and international organizations whose purpose is to support people in small business. Some of these organizations offer education information, contacts, and resources. Others provide benefits such as group insurance rates and discounts on products. Many of these business resource organizations offer information free of charge — but be sure to check. For specialized business support organizations, please refer to the Encyclopedia of Associations.

Academy for Health Services Marketing
250 S. Walker Drive, Suite 200
Chicago, IL 60606
(312) 648-0536

American Business Assoc.
292 Madison Avenue
New York, NY 10017
(212) 949-5900

American Business Women's Assoc.
9100 Ward Parkway, Box 8728
Kansas City, MO 64114
(816) 361-6621

American Entrepreneurs Assoc.
2311 Pontius Avenue
Los Angeles, CA 90064
(213) 478-0437

American Federation of Small Business
407 S. Dearborn Street
Chicago, IL 60605
(312) 427-0207

American Management Assoc.
135 W. 50th Street
New York, NY 10020
(212) 586-8100

American Marketing Assoc.
2505 S. Wacker Drive, Suite 200
Chicago, IL 60606
(312) 645-0536

American Self-Marketing Assoc.
Old Chelsea Station Box 2016
New York, NY 10011
(212) 620-7444

American Small Business Assoc.
P.O. Box 612663
Dallas, TX 75261
(800) 227-1037

American Society of Independent Business
777 Main Street, Suite 1600
Forth Worth, TX 76102
(817) 870-1880

Assoc. of Small Business Development Centers
1313 Farnam, Suite 132
Omaha, NE 68182
(402) 595-2387

Best Employers Assoc.
4201 Birch Street
Newport Beach, CA 92660
(714) 756-6100

Center for Entrepreneurial Management
1615 H Street NW
Washington, DC 20062
(202) 463-5901

Center for International Private Enterprise
1615 H Street NW
Washington, DC 20062
(202) 463-5901

Chexchange Network
P.O. Box 21697
Columbus, OH 21697
(614) 292-4985

Coalition of Women in Nat'l & Int'l Business
P.O. Box 950
Boston, MA 02119
(617) 265-5269

Continental Assoc. of Resolute Employers
101 Petaluma Boulevard N
Petaluma, CA 94952
(707) 778-8600

Council of Better Business Bureaus
1515 Wilson Boulevard
Arlington, VA 22209
(703) 276-0100

Entrepreneurs of America
2020 Pennsylvania Avenue NW, Suite 224
Washington, DC 20006
(800) 533-2665

Entrepreneurship Institute
3592 Corporate Drive, Suite 112
Columbus, OH 43231
(614) 895-1153

Health Insurance Assoc. of America
1025 Connecticut Avenue NW, Suite 1200
Washington, DC 20036

Insurance Information Institute
110 Williams Street
New York, NY 10038
(212) 669-9200

International Assoc. of Business
701 Highlander Boulevard, Suite 200
Arlington, VA 76015
(703) 465-2922

International Council for Small Business
St. Louis University
3674 Lindell Boulevard
St. Louis, MO 63108
(314) 658-3896

National Alliance of Small Business
1825 Eye Street NW, Suite 400
Washington, DC
20077-2740

National Assoc. for Business Organizations
P.O. Box 30149
Baltimore, MD 21270
(301) 446-8070

National Assoc. for Female Executives (NAFE)
127 W. 24th Street
New York, NY 10011
(212) 645-0770

National Assoc. for the Cottage Industry
P.O. Box 14460
Chicago, IL 60614
(312) 472-9116

National Assoc. for the Self-Employed (NASE)
2328 Gravel Road
Ft. Worth, TX 76118
(800) 827-9990

National Assoc. of Private Enterprise
P.O. Box 470398
Ft. Worth, TX 76147
(817) 870-1971

Nat'l Assoc. of Women Business Owners (NAWBO)
600 S. Federal Street, Suite 400
Chicago, IL 60605
(312) 345-2330

National Business Assoc.
15770 N. Dallas Parkway, Suite 260
Dallas, TX 75248
(214) 991-5381

Nat'l Federation of Independent Business (NFIB)
600 Maryland Ave. S.W., Suite 700
Washington, DC 20024-2567
(202) 554-9000

National Insurance Consumer's Organization
121 N. Payne Street
Alexandria, VA 22314
(703) 549-8050

National Small Business Assoc.
1604 K Street NW
Washington, DC 20006
(202) 293-8830

National Small Business Benefits Assoc.
9933 Lawler Avenue #210
Skokie, IL 70077
(312) 679-1499

National Small Business United
1155 15th Street NW, Suite 710
Washington, DC 20005
(202) 293-8830

Natural Marketing Assoc.
22704 Ventura Boulevard
Woodland Hills, CA 91364
(818) 702-0888

Network of Small Business
5420 Mayfield Road, Suite 205
Lyndhurst, OH 44124
(216) 442-5000

Service Corps of Retired Executives (SCORE)
1825 Connecticut Avenue NW, Suite 503
Washington, DC 20009
(800) 368-5855
(202) 653-6279

Small Business Assistance Center
P.O. Box 1441
Worcester, MA 01601
(508) 756-3513

Small Business Legislative Council
1025 Vermont Avenue NW, Suite 1201
Washington, DC 20005
(202) 639-8500

Small Business Network
P.O. Box 30149
Baltimore, MD 21270
(301) 466-8070

Small Business Service Bureau
554 Main Street, Box 1441
Worcester, MA 01601-1441
(508) 756-3513

Small Business Support Center Assoc.
8811 Westheimer Road #210
Houston, TX 77063-3617

Support Services Alliance
P.O. Box 130
Schoharie, NY 12157
(518) 295-7966

U.S. Chamber of Commerce
1615 H Street NW
Washington, DC 20062
(800) 638-6582
(202) 659-6000

U.S. Department of Commerce
Business Assistance
Washington, DC 20230
(202) 377-3176

U.S. Department of Labor
200 Constitution Avenue NW
Washington, DC 20210

U.S. Department of the Treasury
Internal Revenue Service
P.O Box 25866
Richmond, VA 23289
(800) 829-3676
(202) 566-2041

U.S. Small Business Administration (SBA)
1441 L Street NW
Washington, DC 20062
(800) 368-5855
(202) 653-6822

• PROFESSIONAL ASSOCIATIONS •

This register contains the major national and international healing arts professional associations. The total list including the specialized, auxiliary, and local branches of professional associations numbers in the thousands. If you are interested in discovering the scope of the healing arts field or learning more about any particular association, look through the "Health and Medical" section of the Encyclopedia of Associations.

Academy of Scientific Hypnotherapy
P.O. Box 12041
San Diego, CA 92112
(619) 427-6225

Acupuncture Assoc. Int'l
2330 S. Brentwood Boulevard
St. Louis, MO 63144
(314) 961-2300

Alliance of Massage Therapists
226 W. 26th Street
New York, NY 10001

American Acupuncture Assoc.
4622 Kissena Boulevard
Flushing, NY 11355
(718) 886-4431

American Alliance of Massage Professionals
3108 Route 10 West
Denville, NJ 07834
(201) 989-8941

American Aromatherapy Assoc.
3384 S. Robertson Place
Los Angeles, CA 90034
(800) 669-9514

American Aromatherapy Assoc.
P.O. Box 1222
Fair Oaks, CA 95628

American Art Therapy Assoc.
1202 Allanson Road
Mundelein, IL 60060
(312) 949-6064

American Assoc. for Counseling & Development
5999 Stuenson Avenue
Alexandria, VA 22304
(800) 545-2223

American Assoc. for Marriage & Family Therapy
1717 K Street NW #407
Washington, DC 20006
(202) 429-1825

American Assoc. for Music Therapy
P.O. Box 27177
Philadelphia, PA 19118
(215) 242-4450

American Assoc. for Rehabilitation Therapy
P.O. Box 93
North Little Rock, AR 72115

American Assoc. for Therapeutic Humor
1441 Shermer Road, Suite 110
Northbrook, IL 60062
(312) 291-0211

American Assoc. of Ayurvedic Medicine
P.O. Box 541
Lancaster, MA 01523
(508) 368-1818

American Assoc. of Entrepreneurial Dentists
420 Magazine Street
Tupelo, MS 33801
(601) 842-1036

American Assoc. of Equine Practitioners
P.O. Box 55248
Lexington, KY 40504
(606) 233-0147

American Assoc. of Feline Practitioners
1362 Trinity Drive, Suite D-2205
Los Alamos, NM 87541
(505) 662-5682

American Assoc. of Healthcare Consultants
11208 Waples Mill Road, Suite 109
Fairfax, VA 22030
(703) 691-1141

American Assoc. of Homeopathic Pharmacists
P.O. Box 2273
Falls Church, VA 22042
(703) 532-3237

American Assoc. of Hypnotherapists
7117 Farnam Street
Omaha, NE 68132
(402) 397-1500

American Assoc. of Naturopathic Physicians
P.O. Box 2579
Kirkland, WA 98083

American Assoc. of Nutrition Consultants
1641 E. Sunset Road, B117
Las Vegas, NV 89119
(702) 361-1132

American Assoc. of Oriental Healing Arts
P.O. Box 718
Jamaica Plain, MA 02130
(617) 236-5867

American Assoc. of Professional Hypnotherapists
P.O. Box 731
McLean, VA 22101
(703) 448-9623

American Center of Chinese Medical Sciences
7420 Brickyard Road
Potomac, MD 20854

American Chiropractic Assoc.
1701 Clarendon Boulevard
Arlington, VA 22209
(202) 276-8800

American College of Nurse Midwives
Education Director
1522 K Street, NW, Suite 100
Washington, DC 20005
(202) 289-0171

American Dance Therapy Assoc.
2000 Century Plaza, Suite 108
Columbus, MO 21044
(301) 997-4040

American Dental Assistants Assoc.
919 N. Michigan Avenue, Suite 3400
Chicago, IL 60611
(312) 664-3327

American Dental Assoc.
211 E. Chicago Avenue
Chicago, IL 50511
(312) 440-2500

American Dental Hygienists' Assoc.
444 Michigan Avenue, Suite 3400
Chicago, IL 60611
(312) 440-8900

American Foundation for Alternative Health Care
25 Landfield Avenue
Monticello, NY 12701
(914) 794-8181

American Foundation for Homeopathy
706 Edgewood Road
San Mateo, CA 94402
(415) 342-0815

American Healing Assoc.
811 Ridge Drive
Glendale, CA 91206

American Holistic Medical Assoc.
4101 Lake Boone Trail #201
Raleigh, NC 27607

American Holistic Nurses Assoc.
1100 Raleigh Bldg. Five W. Hargett Street
Raleigh, NC 27601
(919) 821-0071

American Holistic Veterinary Medical Assoc.
2214 Old Emmorton Road
Bel Air, MD 21014
(301) 838-7778

American Horticultural Therapy Assoc.
9220 Wightman Road, Suite 300
Gaithersburg, MD 20879
(301) 948-3010

American Hypnosis Assoc.
18607 Ventura Boulevard, Suite 310
Tarzana, CA 91355
(818) 344-4464

American Int'l Reiki Assoc.
2210 Wilshire Boulevard, Suite 831
Santa Monica, CA 90403
(213) 394-6220

American Kinesiotherapy Assoc.
259-08 148 Road
Rosedale, NY 11422
(718) 276-0721

American Massage Therapy Assoc.
1130 W. North Shore Avenue
Chicago, IL 60626-4618
(212) 761-2682

American Medical Assoc.
515 N. State Street
Chicago, IL 60610
(231) 264-5481

American Mental Health Counselors Assoc.
5999 Stevenson Avenue
Alexandria, VA 22304
(703) 823-9800

American Naprapathic Assoc.
5913 W. Montrose Avenue
Chicago, IL 60634
(312) 685-6020

American Natural Hygiene Society
P.O. Box 30630
Tampa, FL 33630
(813) 855-6607

American Nurses' Assoc.
2420 Pershing Road
Kansas City, MO 64108
(816) 474-5720

American Nutritional Medical Assoc.
P.O. Box 25113
Colorado Springs, CO 80936
(719) 591-2659 (303) 341-0084

American Occupational Therapy Assoc.
1383 Piccard Drive, Suite 301
Rockville, MD 20850-4375
(301) 948-9626

American Oriental Bodywork Therapy Assoc.
50 Maple Place
Manhasset, NY 11030
(516) 365-5025

American Osteopathic Assoc.
142 E. Ontario Street
Chicago, IL 60611
(312) 280-5800

American Physical Therapy Assoc.
1111 N. Fairfax Street
Alexandria, VA 22314
(703) 684-2782

American Polarity Therapy Assoc.
P.O. Box 1517
Arlington, MA 02174
(617) 776-6690

American Psychiatric Assoc.
1400 K Street, NW
Washington, DC 20005
(202) 682-6000

American Psychological Assoc.
1200 17th Street, NW
Washington, DC 20036
(202) 955-7600

American Public Health Assoc.
1015 15th Street NW
Washington, DC 20005
(202) 789-5600

American Rehabilitation Counseling Assoc.
5999 Stevenson Drive
Alexandria, VA 22304
(703) 823-9800

American Shiatsu Assoc.
P.O. Box 718
Jamaica Plain, MA 02130
(617) 522-0251

American Society of Clinical Hypnosis
2250 E. Devon Avenue, Suite 336
Des Plaines, IL 60018
(708) 297-3317

American Society of Pastoral & Wellness Counselors
P.O. Box 66
Parker, CO 80134

American Therapeutic Recreation Assoc.
P.O. Box 15215
Hattiesburg, MS 39402
(601) 264-3168

American Veterinary Medical Assoc.
930 N. Meacham Road
Schaumberg, IL 60196
(708) 605-8070

Associated Bodywork & Massage Professionals
P.O. Box 1869
Evergreen, CO 80439
(303) 674-8478

Assoc. for Applied Psycophysiology & Biofeedback
10200 W. 44th Avenue, Suite304
Wheat Ridge, CO 80033
(303) 420-2902

Assoc. for Birth Psychology
444 E. 82nd Street
New York, NY 10028
(212) 988-6617

Assoc. for Equine Massage
Box 5, Site 9, R.R. #8
Edmonton, Alberta T5L 4H8
Canada

Assoc. for Infant Massage
79th Street Boat Basin Box
New York, NY 10084

Assoc. for Past-Life Research and Therapy
P.O. Box 20151
Riverside, CA 92516
(714) 784-1570

Assoc. for the Advancement of Sports Potential
P.O. Box 185
Unionville, PA 19375
(800) 223-7014
(215) 793-1881

Assoc. of Massage Therapists
18 A Spit Road
Mosmman, New South Wales
Australia

Assoc. of Natural Health Practitioners
4 Cunrow Street
Elizabethfield
South Australia 5113

Assoc. of Remedial Masseurs
22 Sturt Street
Ryde 2112
Australia

Assoc. of Wholistic Practitioners
2917 Shady Avenue
Pittsburgh, PA 15217

Australasian Society of Myotherapy
P.O. Box 43
Mitcham, Victoria 3132
Australia

Australian Traditional Medicine Society
120 Blaxland Road, Suite 3
Ryde, New South Wales
Australia

Australian Traditional Medicine Society
78 Colin Street
West Perth
West Australia 6000

Bodywork & Wellness Therapies Assoc.
P.O. Box 60323
Oklahoma City, OK 73146-0323

British Columbia Massage Practitioners
2256 West 4th Avenue
Vancouver, British Columbia V6K 1N8
Canada

C.J. Jung Foundation
28 E. 39th Street
New York, NY 10016
(212) 697-6430

Canadian Sports Massage Assoc.
P.O. Box 159 Station P
Toronto, Ontario M5F 2JO
Canada

Committee for Freedom of Choice in Medicine
1180 Walnut Avenue
Chula Vista, CA 92011
(619) 429-8200

Common Boundary, Inc.
7005 Florida Street
Chevy Chase, MD 20815
(301) 652-9495

Council on Chiropractic Education
4401 Westown Parkway, Suite 120
West Des Moisnes, IA 50285
(515) 226-9001

Council on Chiropractic Physiological Therapeutics
203 N. Holmes Avenue
Idaho Falls, ID 83401
(208) 522-2591

Cranial Academy
1140 W. 8th Street
Meridan, ID 83401
(208) 888-1201

Dr. Edward Bach Healing Society
644 Merrick Road
Lynbrook, NY 11563
(516) 593-2206

Feldenkrais Guild
11450 W. 99th Street
Shawnee Mission, KS 66214-2461

Flotation Tank Assoc.
P.O. Box 1396
Grass Valley, CA 95945
(916) 432-3794

Flower Essence Society
P.O. Box 459
Nevada City, CA 95959
(916) 265-9163

Foot Reflexology Awareness Assoc.
P.O. Box 7622
Mission Hills, CA 91346

Foundation for the Advancement of Chiropractic Tenets &
Sciences
1110 N. Glebe Road, Suite 1000
Arlington, VA 22201
(703) 528-5000

Gerson Institute
P.O. Box 430
Bonita, CA 92002
(619) 267-1150

Healing Arts Assoc.
408 Pleasant Hill Road
Owings Mills, MD 21117

Hellerwork Practitioners Assoc.
P.O. Box 3278
Truckee, CA 95734

Holistic Dental Assoc.
4801 Richmond Square
Oklahoma City, OK 73118
(405) 840-5600

Homeopathic Council for Research & Education
50 Park Avenue
New York, NY 10016
(212) 684-2290

Hunter Masseurs Assoc.
15 Alliance Street
East Maitland, New South Wales
Australia 2323
(417) 831-3188

IDEA: Assoc. for Fitness Professionals
6190 Cornerstone Court E., Suite 204
San Diego, CA 92121
(619) 535-8979

Int'l Academy of Myodontics
800 Airport Boulevard
Doylestown, PA 18901
(215) 345-1149

Int'l Academy of Preventive Medicine
P.O. Box 5832
Lincoln, NE 68505

Int'l Alliance of Nutri-Medical Assoc.
P.O. Box 25113
Colorado Springs, CO 80936
(303) 745-2554

Int'l Assoc. of Holistic Health Practitioners
3419 Thom Boulevard
Las Vegas, NV 89106
(702) 873-4542

Int'l Assoc. for the Study of Pain
909 NE 43rd Street, Suite 306
Seattle, WA 98105
(206) 547-6409

Int'l Assoc. of Infant Massage Instructors
2350 Bowen Road
Elma, NY 14059-0438
(716) 652-9759

Int'l Assoc. of Professional Natural Hygienists
204 Stambaugh Building
Youngstown, OH 44503
(216) 746-5000

Int'l Assoc. of Radiance Technique
Four Embarcadero Center, Suite 5124
San Francisco, CA 94111

Int'l Assoc. of Specialized Kinesiologists
4121 Glen Field Circle
Las Vegas, NV 89129

Int'l Assoc. of T.C. Pfrimmer Deep Muscle Therapists
P.O. Box 807
Smithfield, NC 27577
(919) 934-0734

Int'l Assoc. of the Healing Arts
2443 Ash Street, Suite D
Palo Alto, CA 94306

Int'l Foundation for Homeopathy
2366 Eastlake, E #301
Seattle, WA 98102
(206) 324-8230

Int'l Guild of Hypnotists
410 S. Michigan Avenue, Suite 210
Chicago, IL 60605
(312) 939-0951

Int'l Institute of Reflexology
P.O. Box 12642
St. Petersburg, FL 33733-2642
(813) 343-4811 West Coast: (619) 589-1150

Int'l Institute for Bioenergetics
144 E. 36th Street
New York, NY 10016
(212) 532-7742

Int'l Macrobiotic Shiatsu Assoc.
1122 M. Street
Eureka, CA 95501-2442
(707) 445-2290

Int'l Movement Therapy Assoc.
P.O. Box 3702
Stanford, CA 94309-3702

Int'l Myomassethics Federation
5188 Picadilly Circle
Westminster, CA 92683
(800) 338-8950 · (714) 897-5980

Int'l Shiatsu Assoc.
35 North Cass Avenue
Westmont, IL 60559
(312) 960-4050

Int'l Society for Medical & Psychological Hypnosis
1991 Broadway #18B
New York, NY 10023
(212) 874-5290

Int'l Society of Alternative Health Professionals
P.O. Box 15882
Phoenix, AZ 85060

Int'l Society of Naturopathy
1434 Fremont Avenue
Los Altos, CA 94022
(415) 967-1232

Int'l Society of Orthobionomy
P.O. Box 7750
Berkeley, CA 94707

Int'l Veterinary Acupuncture Society
R.D. #4 Box 216
Chester Springs, PA 19425
(215) 827-7742

Japan Holistic Medical Society
Artere Shinjuku #1011
8-14-17 Nishi Shinjuku, Tokyo
Japan 16

Kaye Rive Educational Institute
259 Soutpansberg
Rietondale Pretoria 0084
South Africa

Kushi Foundation
17 Station Street
Brookline, MA 02147
(617) 738-0045

Massage Therapy Assoc. of British Columbia
Box 442
Westbrook, BC V0H 2A0
Canada

Masseurs Assoc. of Saskatchewan
3036 Albert Street
Regina, Saskatchewan S4S 3N7
Canada

Midwives Alliance of North America
600 Fifth St
Monett, MO 65708

Mercian Practitioners Assoc.
941 S. Havanna
Aurora, CO 80012
(303) 341-0083

Milton H. Erickson Foundation
3603 N. 24th Street
Phoenix, AZ 85016
(602) 956-6196

Nat'l Assoc. for Drama Therapy
300 E. 34th Street, Box 302
New York, NY 10016
(212) 689-2179

Nat'l Assoc. for Music Therapy
505 11th Street SE
Washington, DC 20003
(202) 543-6864

Nat'l Assoc. for Triggerpoint Myotherapy
3900 Eubank Boulevard NE
Albuqurque, NM 87111
(505) 294-4376

Nat'l Assoc. of Neuro Linguistic Programming
310 N. Alabama, Suite A100
Indianapolis, IN 46204
(317) 636-6509

Nat'l Assoc. of Nurse Massage Therapists
P.O. Box 67
Tuckahoe, NY 10707
(914) 961-3251

Nat'l Assoc. of Optometrists & Opticians
18903 S. Miles Road
Cleveland, OH 44128
(216) 475-8925

Nat'l Center for Homeopathy
1500 Massachusetts Avenue NW, Suite 42
Washington, DC 20005
(202) 223-6182

Nat'l Coalition of Arts Therapies Assoc.
505 11th Street SE
Washington, DC 20003
(202) 543-6864

Nat'l Guild of Hypnotists
P.O. Box 308
Merrimack, NH 03054
(603) 429-9438

Nat'l Nurses in Business Assoc.
4286 Redwood Highway, Suite 252
San Rafael, CA 94903
(707) 763-6021

Nat'l Rehabilitation Counseling Assoc.
633 S. Washington Street
Alexandria, VA 22314
(703) 836-7677

Nat'l Society of Hypnotherapists
2175 NW 86th Street, Suite 6A
Des Moisnes, IA 50322
(515) 270-2280

Nat'l Therapeutic Recreation Society
3101 Park Center Drive
Alexandria, VA 22302
(703) 820-4940

Natural Food Assoc.
P.O. Box 210
Athens, TX 75551
(214) 796-3612

Natural Health Society of Australia
541 High Street, Suite 21
Penrith, New South Wales 2750
Australia

New Zealand Assoc. of Therapeutic Massage
P.O. Box 375
Hamilton
New Zealand

North American Academy of Musculoskeletal Medicine
2875 Northwind Drive #207
E. Lansing, MI 48823
(517) 337-2280

North American Society of Teachers of the Alexander
Technique
P.O. Box 806, Ansonia Station
New York, NY 10023-9998
(212) 866-5640

Nurses in Transition
P.O. Box 104
Glencoe, CA 95232

Ontario Massage Therapy Assoc.
456 Danforth Ave
Toronto, Ontario M4K 1P4
Canada

Orthobionomy Assoc.
P.O. Box 70384
Seattle, WA 98107

Ovulation Method Teachers Assoc.
P.O. Box 10-1780
Anchorage, AK 99510
(907) 264-4785

Personal Fitness & Bodyworkers Assoc.
7 Pine Knoll
Lenox, MA 01240
(413) 637-2860

Professional Massage & Remedial Therapy Society
GPO Box 1886
Adelaide
South Australia 5001

Queensland Assoc. of Massage Therapists
11 Maple Street
Wavel Heights, Queensland 4012
Australia

Radix Institute
Route 2, Box 89-A
Granbury, TX 76048
(817) 326-5670

Radix Teacher's Assoc.
2227 Wilton Drive
Ft. Lauderdale, FL 33305
(305) 563-9030

Reflexology Assoc. of Canada
384 Alper Street
Richmond Hill, Ontario L4C 2Z4
Canada

Reiki Alliance
East 33135 Canyon Road
Cataldo, ID 83810

Rolf Institute
Box 1868
Boulder, CO 80306
(303) 449-5903

Rosen Method Professional Assoc.
2315 Prince Street
Berkeley, CA 94705

Serendipity Assoc. for Research & Implementation of
Holistic Health & World Peace
7010 Casa Lane #5
Lemon Grove, CA 92045
(619) 697-9711

Shiatsu Practitioner Assoc.
2309 Main Street
Santa Monica, CA 90405

Shiatsu Therapeutic Assoc. of America
602 Kailua Road #205-B
Kailua, HI 96734

Shiatsu Therapy Assoc. of Ontario
P.O. Box 695, Station P
Toronto, Ontario M5S 2Y4
Canada

Society for Clinical & Experimental Hypnosis
128-A Kings Park Drive
Liverpool, NY 13090
(315) 682-7299

Society of Natural Therapists & Researchers
7 Legrande Street
Freshwater, Queensland 4870
Australia

Soma Practitioners Assoc.
5879 SW 72nd Street #3
Miami, FL 33143-5219

South Australia Masseurs Assoc.
148 Glynburn Road
Tranmere 5073
Australia

Tai Chi Assoc.
4651 Roswell Road, Suite E402
Atlanta, GA 30342
(404) 252-4888
(404) 289-5652

Touch for Health Foundation
1174 N. Lake Avenue
Pasadena, CA 91104-3797
(818) 794-1181

United States Physical Therapy Assoc.
1803 Avon Lane
Arlington Heights, IL 60004

United States Sports Massage Federation
120 East 18th Street
Costa Mesa, CA 92627
(714) 642-0235

Victorian Assoc. of Remedial Masseurs
13 Lyons Nth Street
Ballarat 3350
Australia

West Australian Assoc. of Masseurs
16 Woodchester Road
Nullamara
West Australia 6061

Worldwide Assoc. of Reflexologists
Box 64
Oakville, Manitoba R0H 0Y0
Canada

• IRS & SBA PUBLICATIONS •

Both the Small Business Administration (SBA) and the Internal Revenue Service (IRS) offer publications to help you in the management of your business. The publications from the SBA are modestly priced and give a lot of good information, ideas, and examples. The free publications from the IRS assist you in understanding your legal tax requirements and the correct procedures, as well as offer advice and ideas.

The Small Business Directory (SBA Form 115A) lists their publications and videotapes for managing a successful small business. The Guide To Free Tax Services (IRS Publication 910) lists free publications, free phone service, and tax return filing tips. The following (slightly abbreviated) lists provide the order number, title, and fee, so you can directly order these publications.

SMALL BUSINESS ADMINISTRATION PUBLICATIONS —

P.O. Box 30, Denver, CO 80201-0030
(202) 653-6654 • (800) 368-5855

FINANCIAL MANAGEMENT

FM1	ABC's of Borrowing	1.00
FM2	Profit Costing for Manufacturers	1.00
FM3	Basic Budgets for Profit Planning	.50
FM4	Understanding Cash Flow	.50
FM5	A Venture Capital Primer for Small Business	.50
FM6	Accounting Services for Small Firms	.50
FM7	Analyze Your Records to Reduce Costs	.50
FM8	Budgeting In A Small Business Firm	.50
FM9	Sound Cash Management and Borrowing	.50
FM10	RecordKeeping In A Small Business	1.00
FM11	Simple Breakeven Analysis for Small Stores	1.00
FM12A	Pricing Checklist for Small Retailers	.50
FM13	Pricing Your Products & Services Profitably	1.00

MANAGEMENT & PLANNING

MP1	Effective Business Communications.	.50
MP2	Locating or Relocating Your Business	1.00
MP3	Problems In Managing A Family-Owned Business	.50
MP6	Planning & Goal Setting for Small Business	.50
MP7	Fixing Production Mistakes	.50
MP8	Should You Lease or Buy Equipment	.50
MP9	Business Plans for Retailer	1.00
MP10	Choosing A Retail Location	1.00
MP11	Business Plan for Small Service Firms	.50
MP12	Going Into Business	.50
MP14	How To Get Started With A Small Business Computer	1.00
MP15	The Business Plan for Homebased Business	1.00
MP16	How To Buy or Sell A Business	1.00
MP18	Buying for Retail Stores	1.00
MP19	Small Business Decision Making	1.00
MP20	Business Continuation Plan	1.00
MP21	Developing A Strategic Business Plan	1.00
MP22	Inventory Management	.50
MP23	Techniques for Problem Solving	1.00
MP24	Techniques for Productivity Improvement	1.00
MP25	Selecting The Legal Structure for Your Business	.50
MP26	Evaluating Franchise Opportunities	.50
MP28	Small Business Risk Management Guide	1.00
MP29	Quality Child Care Makes Good Business Sense	2.00

CRIME PREVENTION

CP1	Reducing Shoplifting Losses	.50
CP2	Curtailing Crime – Inside and Out	1.00
CP3	A Small Business Guide to Computer Security	1.00

PERSONNEL MANAGEMENT

PM1	Checklist for Developing A Training Program	.50
PM2	Employees: How to Find and Pay Them	1.00
PM3	Managing Employee Benefits	1.00

NEW PRODUCTS/IDEAS/INVENTIONS

PI1	Ideas Into Dollars	2.00
PI2	Avoiding Patent, Trademark & Copyright Problems	1.00
PI3	Trademarks and Business Goodwill	1.00

MARKETING

DEPARTMENT OF THE TREASURY, INTERNAL REVENUE SERVICE —

Forms Distribution Center, P.O. Box 25866
Richmond, VA 23289 · (800) 829-3676

1	You Rights as a Taxpayer
15	Circular E: Employer's Tax Guide
17	Your Federal Income Tax
334	Tax Guide for Small Business
910	Guide to Free Tax Services - List of free publications
463	Travel, Entertainment, & Gift Expenses
501	Exemptions, Standard Deductions, & Filing Information
502	Medical & Dental Expenses
503	Child and Dependent Care Expenses
504	Tax Information for Divorced or Separated Individuals
505	Tax Withholding & Estimated Tax
508	Educational Expenses
517	Social Security for Members of the Clergy & Religious Workers
520	Scholarships & Fellowships
521	Moving Expenses
523	Tax Information on Selling Your Home
525	Taxable & Nontaxable Income
526	Charitable Contributions
527	Residential Rental Property
529	Miscellaneous Deductions
530	Tax Information for Homeowners
531	Reporting Income from Tips
533	Self-Employment Tax
534	Depreciation
535	Business Expenses
536	Net Operating Losses
537	Installment Sales
541	Tax Information on Partnerships
542	Tax Information on Corporations
544	Sales & Other Dispositions of Assets
545	Interest Expense
547	Nonbusiness Disasters, Casualties & Thefts
550	Investment Income & Expenses
551	Basis of Assets
552	Recordkeeping for Individuals
555	Federal Tax Information on Community Property
556	Examination of Returns, Appeal Rights & Claims for Refund
557	Tax-Empt Status for Your Organization
560	Retirement Plans for the Self-Employed
561	Determining the Value of Donated Property
564	Mutual Fund Distributions
583	Taxpayers Starting a Business
584	Nonbusiness Disaster, Casualty & Theft Loss Workbook
586A	The Collection Process (Income Tax Accounts)
587	Business Use of Your Home
589	Tax Information on S Corporations
590	Individual Retirement Arrangements (IRAs)
594	The Collection Process (Employment Tax Accounts)
596	Earned Income Credit
598	Tax on Unrelated Business Income of Exempt Organizations
907	Tax Information for Persons with Handicaps or Disabilities
908	Bankruptcy and Other Debt Cancellation
909	Alternative Minimum Tax for Individuals
911	Tax Information for Direct Sellers
917	Business Use of a Car
924	Reporting of Real Estate Transactions to IRS
925	Passive Activity and At-Risk Rules
926	Employment Taxes for Household Employers
929	Tax Rules for Children and Dependents
936	Limits on Home Mortgage Interest Deduction
937	Business Reporting

INDEX _____

A _____

Advertising: 48, 72, 78, 81, 84, 86, 87, 97-101, 110, 112-114, 118, 119, 153, 160, 161, 163-166, 185
    classified: 118
    cooperative: 98
    display: 116
    listings: 118
    public relations: 119
    techniques: 118, 119
    word-of-mouth: 48, 57
    yellow pages: 118
see *also* marketing, promotion

Advisors: 172, 177, 192, 196

Affirmations: 3, 29, 40-43

Agreements: 49, 71, 72, 168, 172

Articles: 52, 58, 98, 110, 115, 122, 125, 134, 151, 172, 182, 196

Associates: 21, 71, 72, 117, 126, 179

Attitude: 3, 8, 51, 117, 126, 179

B _____

Balance: 77, 80, 91, 108, 179, 182, 183, 196

Barter: 8, 82, 85, 123, 124, 181

Body Language: 57, 59, 60, 65

Bookkeeping: 21, 82-87, 171, 214-222

Booths: 116

Brochures: 57, 58, 110, 112, 115, 116, 123, 124, 151

Budgets: 153
    see *also* finances

Business Cards: 8, 51, 84, 123

Business Groups: 125

Business Hours: 78, 150

Business Location: 69, 144

Business Name: 68, 69, 123, 140

Business Plan: 28, 40, 67, 68, 72, 87, 113, 139-173, 189, 196

Business Start-Up: 68-70

C _____

Cash Flow: 68, 78, 82, 163-166, 219

Character: 123, 146, 192

Checklist for Starting a Business: 9, 10

Clearing: 11-19, 27, 41, 42, 179, 191, 194, 195
    concept: 11
    dissolving problems: 194
    exercises: 12-19, 194
    techniques: 11

Clerical Staff: 75-77
see *also* employees

Client Files: 28, 39, 80-82, 92, 133, 206-212, 220

Client Retention: 7, 15, 47, 133-135, 206-212

Collage: 29, 30

Commitment: 3, 49, 67, 80, 190, 192

Communication: 8, 48, 49, 53, 54, 67, 71, 76, 77, 180, 182, 192

Competition: 40, 78, 97-99, 102, 106, 107, 109, 110, 112, 114, 150-152, 173

Conditioning: 11, 27, 178, 180

Consistency: 118, 185

Conventions: 98, 116

Credibility: 53, 78, 80, 114-117, 123, 124, 129, 192

Customer Service: 39, 40, 133

D _____

Definition of Business: 144, 145

Delivery: 58, 59, 62, 63

Demonstrations: 59, 62, 98, 103, 110, 115, 120

Differential Advantage: 48, 69, 82, 98, 99, 107, 112, 114, 118, 123, 149

Direct Mail: 110, 115, 117

Documentation: 54, 133, 185, 206-213, 220-222

E _____

Education: 55, 56, 58, 84, 86, 87, 98, 101, 115, 181, 182, 196

Employees: 54, 69-71, 73-77, 90, 92, 182

Employer ID Number: 69

Employment Interviewing: 54

Entrepreneurial Traits: 8

Etiquette: 51, 133, 134

Exhibits: see booths and conventions

Expenses: 71-74, 78-80, 82-84, 86-90, 159, 162-166, 189, 216-218, 221, 222

F _____

Federal Taxes: see *also* taxes

Fees: 78-80, 84, 86, 87, 128, 149, 160, 161, 163-166, 182

Fictitious Name Registration: 69

Finances: 67, 68, 139, 158-166, 191

First Impressions: 57

Follow-up: 129, 133, 134, 188

Follow-through: 41-43

G _____

Gift Certificates: 57

Goal Setting: 27-41, 181

Goodwill: 48-52, 75, 77, 80, 83, 133

H _____

High Priority Activities: 40, 183, 184, 189, 200

I

Image: 47-52, 69, 75, 99, 106, 109, 123, 146, 178, 183, 191

Independent Contractor: 67, 78, 79

Insurance Billing: 91, 210

Insurance Coverage: 70

Integrity: 43, 49, 52

Internal Revenue Service: 69, 73, 74, 80, 88-90, 181

Introductions: 57, 58, 62

L

Leasing: 69

Letters: 115, 117, 118, 121, 172, 188

Licensing: 67-69; see *also* permits

Liability: 70, 74, 83, 84, 88, 160, 180

Logistics: 71, 72; see *also* operations

Logo: 84, 118, 123

M

Management: 67-94

Marketing: 58, 97-135, 146-156, 185, 189
    analysis: 99, 110-112, 132, 151
    assessment: 110, 113, 152, 156
    budget: 153, 154
    concept: 97, 98
    plan: 99, 114, 146-156
    target marketing: 101-105
    techniques: 114-124, 133-135, 187, 191
see *also* advertising, differential advantage, positioning and promotion

Mentors: 126, 130

Motivation: 47, 133, 134, 177, 181, 193, 194

N

Networking: 54, 57-59, 78, 84, 126-132, 161, 172, 182, 196
    concept: 126
    groups: 127, 128

Newsletter: 117

O

Operations: 167-171

Ordinances: 47, 71

P

Partnership: 70-72, 88

Permits: 69

Philosophy: 49, 58, 75, 92, 93, 108, 123, 127, 128, 140, 146, 192

Photographs: 116, 117, 124

Policies: 51, 68, 70, 76, 77, 91, 94, 134, 157, 167, 168

Positioning: 101, 106-109, 134, 149; see *also* marketing

Presentations: 60, 98, 115, 116

Press Releases: 58, 110, 119-122, 125

Printed Marketing Material: 115, 117, 123, 124

Procedures: 67, 69, 77, 80, 91-94, 167, 169, 182

Procrastination: 178, 179

Professional Associations: 127, 227-232; see *also* networking

Professionalism: 48-52, 114

Promotion: 8, 48, 56, 57, 72, 79, 84, 86, 87, 97-101, 110-112, 114-116, 119, 125, 153, 154, 160, 161, 163-166, 168, 182, 185
see *also* advertising and marketing

Public Relations: 114, 119-133

Public Speaking: 31, 48, 59-63, 97, 98, 110, 119, 125

R

Referrals: 22, 48, 52, 110, 115, 125-127, 134, 189, 206

Resumes: 55, 56

Risk Taking: 190, 191

S

Scope: 20-24, 27, 48, 71, 73, 101, 115, 118, 126, 139

Self-Employment: 8-10, 71, 72, 83, 88

Self-Esteem: 56, 180

Self Management: 41, 67, 177-196

Small Business Administration: 8, 68, 233, 234

S.O.A.P. Charting: 80, 81

Strategic Planning: 38-41, 113, 180, 203-205

Stress: 53, 58, 103, 120, 121, 180-183

Success: 3, 8, 12, 15, 29, 32, 38, 43, 48, 52, 55, 57, 74, 86, 108, 114, 123, 126, 139, 169, 173, 177-179, 181-185, 190-192

Supplies: 8, 30, 51, 70, 72-84, 86, 87, 91, 116, 129, 145, 150, 160-166, 170, 178, 181

T

Target Marketing: 101-105

Taxes: 21, 67, 73, 78, 79, 83, 87-90, 160, 161, 163-166, 213, 220-222

Telephone: 42, 54, 84, 86, 87, 118, 122, 129, 157, 160-166, 196

Time Management: 177, 180, 181, 195, 200-202

Tracking: 41, 82, 177, 185-189, 200, 202

V, W, Z

Visual Aids: 60, 62

Visualization: 29, 30, 41

Venture Capital: 68

Wheel of Life: 4, 5, 28, 32, 199

Word-of-Mouth Promotion: 48, 57

Zoning: 68, 69

AFTERWORD

Business Mastery is the culmination of more than thirteen years of love and hard work. I started my consulting practice in 1978 and after six months I decided to change my focus and work full time as a massage practitioner. Approximately another six months passed and I realized that I needed a change. I loved working with people and supporting them in achieving their health goals, and I really missed the intellectual stimulation that I got from consulting. So, I embarked on my new journey of a dual career. I often found it difficult to juggle the two careers. My massage persona was very different from "Cherie the business woman".

In 1979 I developed a booklet for use in my consulting practice. I had discovered that I was asking my clients a lot of the same initial questions. One of my clients was so enthused about the booklet that he said he would help me get it published. All I had to do was write down all of the verbal instructions that I gave during sessions. At first that task seemed insurmountable because I did not consider myself a writer. I did a lot of work on the manual. Alas, in the meantime the client disappeared and the manual was never finished.

Then in 1980 I was trained as a rebirther. This was so exciting to me because now, not only did I have such a powerful clearing technique, but also a bridge between the worlds of massage and consulting. I continued my three pronged career until we moved to Tucson in 1983. At that point (and to this date) I decided to concentrate my attention on building a successful consulting practice and have massage and rebirthing be my avocations.

In 1987 I was asked to write an article for a magazine. I felt honored and scared. (Remember, I wasn't a "writer".) Well, I pushed myself and wrote the article. I got wonderful feedback. I also discovered that I really enjoy writing! Since then I have written numerous articles for magazines and journals.

I have always been very certain that I am on this planet to make a major contribution. I am dedicated to supporting people in having their lives be the way THEY want them to be. That theme has been at the core of all of my career and business choices. I view life from a holistic standpoint. I believe in balance.

One of my major goals is elevating the status of the healing arts. To do this, practitioners need to become business professionals. At first my role in this effort was through teaching at the Desert Institute for the Healing Arts, giving seminars on effective business habits and consulting with healing arts practitioners. But I realized that I was only reaching a limited number of people. I decided that the best way for me to support this cause was to write this book.

I welcome any comments you may have about the content, style or layout of this book. I will do my best to incorporate your suggestions in subsequent editions of Business Mastery.

I wish you great happiness, health, prosperity, success and balance!

OTHER OFFERINGS _____

BUSINESS CONSULTING —

I am pleased to offer a special price on consulting services to the purchasers of *Business Mastery*. You will receive a thirty percent discount off of my current fees. I am available for on-site services or by telephone appointment.

BUSINESS PLAN REVIEWS —

If you would like your business plan reviewed, please send us either a typed or legibly printed copy of your business plan along with a check for $75.00 to Sohnen-Moe Associates, 3906 West Ina Road, Suite 200-348, Tucson, AZ 85741-2295. We will return your business plan along with our recommendations and comments. If you want your business plan critiqued (in addition to the review, it includes a financial analysis), please call us at (602) 743-3936 for the appropriate fee for this service.

THE BUSINESS MASTERY WORKSHOP —

The Business Mastery Workshop is an exciting, interactive workshop where you make a quantitative shift in your relationship to your business. The focus is supporting you in living your life and running your business from your values. You will clarify your vision and then learn specific, creative, proven techniques for actualizing your goals. Some of the subjects reviewed in this book are best learned in a personal or workshop setting (e.g., presentation skills, brochure design, etc.).

The Business Mastery Workshop also allows you the opportunity to get feedback on your specific concerns. Topics include business management, increasing client retention, creating effective marketing strategies, getting publicity, networking, diversification, cooperative marketing, self management, developing a dynamic self-introduction, designing promotional materials, educating your clients, increasing your profits, presenting yourself powerfully, and keeping balance.

The Business Mastery Workshop inspires powerful insights and results for seasoned business professionals as well as those just embarking in their field. We are continually adding dates to our workshop schedule, so please call us for current dates and locations. This workshop is also available as an in-house program for your organization, school, or professional association. Please contact us if you would like to sponsor the Business Mastery Workshop.

THE PRESENTATION SKILLS WORKSHOP —

Public speaking is the key to expanding your business! People become your clients out of their experience of you. Public speaking increases your visibility in the community, educates the public about the benefits of your services, and establishes your credibility.

The Presentation Skills Workshop provides you with the skills to speak powerfully and confidently from informal one-on-one contacts to formal group presentations. This exciting program is fast paced, participative and fun.

Discover how to increase your comfort when speaking in public; build your communication strengths; create a presentation outline; expand your practice through educating the public; enhance your delivery through your voice and body language; design a powerful self–introduction; involve and motivate your audience; research, organize and practice your presentations; incorporate demonstrations and audio-visuals; and develop effective workshop marketing techniques.

VALUE ORIENTED MARKETING —

Have you ever wondered why some people seem naturally successful with their careers while others struggle? We've all been told that if you do what you love, then money will easily flow to you. Unfortunately, it's not quite so simple. You need to take action to foster success.

Discover how to expand your practice by using proven techniques that integrate your values into your business. Effective marketing is the cornerstone to a successful practice. Marketing involves all of the business activities done on a daily basis to attract potential clients to utilize your services. Thriving practices combine a good mixture of promotion, advertising, and public relations. This highly interactive workshop focuses on increasing your success by integrating **YOU** into your marketing. Discover how to clarify your differential advantage, determine your position statement, target your market and utilize effective promotional strategies.

Even if you are doing well in your practice, you will leave this workshop knowing how to increase the impact of your marketing in your print materials, presentations, networking and advertising. You will also discover how to get free media coverage and expand your visibility through creative marketing techniques and cooperative marketing.

THERAPEUTIC COMMUNICATION SKILLS —

Effective Communication with Clients, the Public and Other Health Care Providers. Excellent communication skills are integral to a successful practice. As therapists, we need to be able to adapt our style as well as vocabulary when talking with different people such as clients, other health care providers and the general public. The more you enhance your communication abilities, the easier it becomes to build your practice, develop professional affiliations, and retain clients.

In this workshop you will learn the keys to effective therapeutic communications and interpersonal interactions. We cover client interactions: how to develop rapport, do great intake interviews (elicit appropriate information, using "buzz" words, understand non-verbal cues), design treatment plans, get feedback during sessions, and empower your clients in their well-being. We also explore ways to build professional alliances: developing a team approach to wellness, designing a descriptive promotional package, and marketing to physicians and other primary health care providers.

Professional Development Resources Catalog —

We want you to be successful! So, we've assembled a catalog of products to assist you in developing the "business" part of your business. Too often we invest the majority of our time and money enhancing our technical skills and ignore developing our business acumen.

Our goal is to provide you with convenient, affordable access to state-of-the-art information and products for your professional development. We are dedicated to supporting other small businesses. Many of the items we carry are written or produced by individuals like yourself — and it may be awhile before their products are widely available. The following pages contain a sampling of the items we stock.

The Art of Supportive Leadership

By J. Donald Walters   **$7.95**   **103 pages**   **5 x 7**   **#B160**
This book is a new approach to leadership, one that views leadership in terms of shared accomplishment rather than of personal advancement. It is an invaluable handbook for business owners, managers, officeholders of professional associations, teachers, parents, politicians, and anyone else who needs to work with people to get things done.

Athletic Ritual

By Kate Montgomery   **$24.95**   **165 pages**   **8.5 x 11**   **#B180**
Named the "Secret Weapon," this book is a proven system designed to increase performance, stamina and energy, and shorten recovery time. A certified sports massage therapist's system to aid athletes, coaches, and others to create their own wholistic program for better health and productivity.   **Quantity Discounts Available**

The Bodywork Entrepreneur: Compiled articles from issues 1-12

Edited by David Palmer   **$24.00**   **215 pages**   **8.5 x 11**   **#B104**
David Palmer took the best articles from his Bodywork Entrepreneur newsletter and compiled them into a book format. These informative and inspiring articles are grouped under related themes such as the nature of business, the structure of business, approaches to the wide diversity of markets available to massage professionals, identity and boundaries as a bodywork professional, and observations on the future of massage.

Bodywork Greeting Cards: "Knowing You is a Touching Experience"

By Suzie Bennett   **25 @ $20.00**   **50 @ $35.00**   **100 @ $65.00**   **200 @ $120.00**   **#S105**
Increase your business by remembering your clients with a bodywork greeting card. Ideal for birthdays, special dates, thank-you notes for referrals, or as a get-well wish. Reactivate old business from those you haven't seen in some time. Cards are 4.5 x 5.5, black-and-white, in a 3-panel fold, printed on a glossy white stock. Create your message on the blank third panel. Verse reads: "Knowing You is a Touching Experience." Envelopes included.

Business Mastery: A Business Planning Guide for Creating A Fulfilling, Thriving Business and Keeping It Successful

By Cherie Sohnen-Moe   **256 pages**   **8.5 x 11**   **Soft Cover $19.95**   **#B102**
   3-Hole Drilled $21.95   **#B202**
Business Mastery is in bookstores, libraries and more than 225 schools worldwide (with many requiring it as a text). This comprehensive guide balances practical business skills with a humanistic approach. It's filled with information and exercises on vital topics including marketing and promotion, client retention, professionalism, referrals, planning, business start-up, choosing advisors, designing promotional material, self management and networking. Also includes a business plan outline, 22 reproducible business templates, a business resource directory, a select register of professional associations and a condensed list of SBA and IRS publications.

CARPAL TUNNEL SYNDROME: PREVENTION AND TREATMENT

BY KATE MONTGOMERY $14.95   64 PAGES   8.5 x 11   #B181

A self-help guide to prevent and treat repetitive motion injury of the hands and arms. A non-surgical solution to improving grip strength, relieving muscle tension in elbows, wrists and hands, and increasing flexibility and mobility.   **Quantity Discounts Available**

CARPAL TUNNEL SYNDROME: THE INVISIBLE THREAT

BY KATE MONTGOMERY $12.95   60-MINUTE AUDIO   #A180

Based on Kate Montgomery's CTS book, this tape focuses on teaching what carpal tunnel syndrome is and how to prevent or manage it. Routine and exercises taught, statistics on the problem reviewed, with the second side of the tape a menu of music to practice to during your daily activities.   **Quantity Discounts Available**

THE COMPLETE BUSINESS MANUAL FOR CANADIAN THERAPISTS

BY M.A. LABRASH $14.95   94 PAGES   8.5 x 11   #B170

Originally developed as an accompaniment to *Business Mastery*, this guide is a must for Canadian therapists! It provides the specific information they need to succeed. The first two sections of the manual are devoted to studying common tax situations, with real-life problems to be worked through. The third section provides information on RRSPs, the new B.C. and Ontario health legislation, the insurance climate in Canada, and tips on how to increase your clients.

CREATIVE MARKETING

BY PATRICIA RASKIN $13.95   90 PAGES   8.5 x 11   #B133

A hands-on workbook approach to marketing with specific examples of the features and benefits of massage therapy to different markets. Includes low-cost and no-cost marketing strategies. Also contains samples of effective policies and many other tips and techniques to help massage therapists more effectively market their practices.

CREATIVE MASSAGE THERAPIST

BY CHARLES HAYES, M.A., L.M.T., A.T.R $19.95   CASSETTE & WORKBOOK   #A170

This is a program of creative unfoldment for professional massage therapists. CMT reveals crucial secrets about WHY imagination is our human "Central Intelligence"; HOW it is vital to your success; WHY it is inseparable to the challenge of the dawning millennium to manifest new messages. This program combines psychology, art therapy, and Native American stories with massage.

FINDING YOUR NICHE...MARKETING YOUR PROFESSIONAL SERVICE

BY B. BRODSKY & J.GEIS $15.95   272 PAGES   8.5 x 11   #B139

Finding Your Niche shows you how to market all kinds of services, from accounting to Zen, dance lessons to therapy sessions. Many professionals find it difficult to "sell themselves", to describe what they do in terms that are attractive to prospective clients. This book addresses these needs and covers the entire marketing process: identifying prospective clients; researching your market; getting known as an authority; conducting a promotion campaign; writing effective ad copy; producing winning flyers and brochures; and how to build sideline careers writing and lecturing.

FREEDOM FROM BACK PAIN — THE MENSENDIECK SYSTEM

BY KAREN A. PERLROTH $29.95   55-MINUTE VHS/42-PAGE BOOKLET   #V130

Recommended by Stanford University Center For Research in Disease Prevention. This award-winning, revolutionary European system of back care teaches why your back hurts, how to fix it yourself and how to keep it pain-free.   **Quantity Discounts Available**

FREEDOM FROM BACK PAIN — THE MENSENDIECK AUDIO

BY KAREN A. PERLROTH $12.95   65-MINUTE AUDIO   #A130
New program applying the Mensendiek System to travelling in the car, sleeping, sitting, working and daily life situations. Includes applied exercises, background information and routines for breathing and posture.   **Quantity Discounts Available**

HANDS HEAL: DOCUMENTATION FOR MASSAGE THERAPY

BY DIANA THOMPSON $14.95   80 PAGES   8.5 x 11   #B160
Hands Heal: Documentation For Massage Therapy, A Guide to SOAP Charting explains and demonstrates all the documentation any bodyworker needs to establish and maintain a system of accurate client/treatment information (as needed by most insurance companies and other health care providers). This step-by-step learning tool is valuable to new practitioners as well as those experienced with filling out insurance reports. Highly recommended regardless of whether or not you work with insurance reimbursement.

HANDS HEAL PROFESSIONAL DOCUMENTATION

BY DIANA THOMPSON   SCHOOL/CLINIC $99.95 #S106A   INDIVIDUAL $19.95   #S106
This packet includes a copy of every form presented in *Hands Heal* and grants reproduction permission to the purchaser. Forms are printed (not copied) on white recycled paper and enclosed in acetate slipcovers for safe storage. The school/clinic package extends reproduction permission to all present and future students/practitioners of one school location or clinic.

HAPPY FLOWERS INSIGHT CARDS

BY SOFTWARE FOR SERENITY $8.99   #P102
The Happy Flowers Insight Cards are a delightful blend of succinct, powerful insights, inspired by Nature. Based on attitudinal healing principles, they are designed to assist people in thinking and feeling healthily and happily. The set includes metaphors, quotations, positive reframes, humor and more. Our clients love to pick a card after a session. Each set consists of 90 double-sided cards on pastel parchment, in alternative colors: rose, champagne, teal, blue, orchid; some illustrated with flower motifs; in a beautiful gold-foil box. In addition to your personal use, these cards make an elegant gift for your clients.

THE INNER MANAGER

BY RON DALRYMPLE, PH.D. $8.95   108 PAGES   5.5 x 8.5   #B108
The Inner Manager: Mastering Business, Home, and Self reveals how you can use your rational, emotional and intuitive resources to successfully manage conflicts, financial worries, family problems and many other aspects of your life, helping you gain the respect and success we all need. This book, told in the form of a simple parable, leads you through an eight-step mind development course that is easy and fun to read. This book integrates the sciences, modern day psychologies, and Eastern/Western philosophies into a powerhouse of pragmatic ideas and techniques designed to help you better manage your life today.

THE INSURANCE REIMBURSEMENT MANUAL FOR BODYWORKERS & MASSAGE PROFESSIONALS

BY CHRISTINE ROSCHE $49.95   220 PAGES   8.5 x 11   #B135
The Insurance Reimbursement Manual is a systematic, concise reference manual that makes the business of insurance billing clearer and easier to understand. This spiral-bound guide contains primary information applicable to bodyworkers of all levels of expertise. In addition to the information on how to process third-party insurance claims and keep correct charts & records, this manual also includes sample forms and describes techniques for establishing effective, profitable business relationships with Medical Doctors, Chiropractors and other health professionals.

Is Your "Net" Working?

BY ANNE BOE & BETTIE YOUNGS   **$22.95 250 PAGES**   **6 x 9**   **#B111**

Is Your "Net" Working is a complete guide to building contacts and career visibility. This book contains practical information and advice on how to develop strong networking skills, measure your current networking techniques, find the hottest professional networks, meet the "right" people, and build a personal network of key contacts. Each chapter contains real-life case studies and exercises to give you "hands-on" training. This book contains everything you need to start and run a network that will help you meet your professional and personal goals.

Is Your Net-Working? Audio Cassettes

BY ANNE BOE   **$25.00**   **4 TAPES**   **#A111**

Learn how to network for customer service and sales success by identifying your preferred networking and sales style. Discover how to communicate and blend your networking style with your client. Become an effective and powerful business networker by building relationships that last, and establishing realistic and achievable career goals. Thus you will stay ahead of the competition, work smarter — not harder, and learn how to add humor to your career success.

Marketing With Newsletters

BY ELAINE FLOYD   **$24.95**   **256 PAGES**   **7.25 x 9.25**   **#B136**

Most forms of advertising are considered inappropriate for health care practitioners, yet a newsletter is viewed by clients as an added service. It's a cost-effective way to stay in touch with clients, while building your image in the community. Increase your practice by producing an informative and promotional publication. Through 13 chapters and over 200 examples, testimonials and cartoons, this easy-to-read book demonstrates how to choose engaging content, write and design an effective newsletter. For current newsletter publishers & those just getting started.

Marketing Without Advertising

BY M. PHILLIPS & S. RASBERRY   **$14.00**   **240 PAGES**   **8.5 x 11**   **#B106**

This book provides you with the philosophical underpinnings for the development of a successful, low-cost marketing plan not based on advertising. Phillips and Rasberry demolish the myth of advertising effectiveness and outline practical steps for marketing your small business. This book is for the business person who is proud of and enjoys providing a quality product or service.

Massage, A Career At Your Fingertips

BY MARTIN ASHLEY   **$19.95**   **292 PAGES**   **7 x 10**   **#B148**

A career reference manual for any would-be or currently practicing bodywork/massage therapist covering guides to laws, associations, schools, companies supplying the profession and extensive reference materials including continuing education programs. Provides insight into the kinds of training, experience and self-examination necessary for the profession.

Money Magnetism

BY J. DONALD WALTERS   **$7.95**   **125 PAGES**   **5 x 7**   **#B161**

This book offers fresh new insights on proven ways of increasing abundance without making it a burden on one's peace of mind. It contains techniques and keys for attracting to yourself the power and success that everyone seeks in life. It is a book about money, but also about a great deal more. Its larger purpose is to help you attract whatever you need in life, when you need it.

"NETWORKING" FOR YOUR PERSONAL & FINANCIAL GROWTH

BY ANNE BOE $ 40.00   50-MINUTE VHS   #V111

. This video guide assists you in finding, developing and nurturing business and social contacts. Learn what networking really is; how to take action now; how to warm up the coldest people; how to grow your own network; how to follow up with clients; how to become a successful networker, friend, business person — and have fun achieving your career success.

NEW MARKETING OPPORTUNITIES

BY SOPHIA TARILA, PH.D. $89.95   428 PAGES   8.5 x 11   #B107

The only trade directory for the metaphysical New Age conscious marketplace. Its purpose is to provide time-saving and easy accessibility to the "consciousness" marketplace by having almost 7000 pertinent names, addresses, phone numbers, and other vital information necessary for the successful marketing of products, publications and services.

NO STRAIN/NO PAIN SERIES

BY KAREN PERLROTH $29.95   30-MINUTE VHS/30-PAGE BOOKLET

WOMEN #V131   MEN #V132   PREGNANCY / CHILDBIRTH #V133   SENIORS #V134

All five programs (based on the Mensendieck System) will help your clients create a healthy back for life: learn to move and exercise safely, enhance athletic performance, improve posture, tone muscles and prevent injury.   **Quantity Discounts Available**

ONE FREE HUG COUPONS

BY SOFTWARE FOR SERENITY   20 COUPONS PER PACK FOR $1.50   #P103

"Good for ONE FREE HUG .... from any participating human being!" Some counselors now recommend 8-12 hugs per day for optimal emotional health. Many of us are "natural huggers", but sometimes people need permission to hug. Our FREE HUG COUPONS encourage everyone to go ahead and do what feels good! These coupons are attractively illustrated and printed double-sided on pink parchment cardstock.

"ON-SITE MASSAGE IN THE WORKPLACE" PROMOTIONAL VIDEO

BY DAVID PALMER $20.00   6-MINUTE VHS   #V104

This marketing tape is a six minute introduction to workplace massage. It begins with an introduction by David Palmer, continues with a video story about a company that employs a full-time on-site massage practitioner, and ends with a summary of why on-site massage in the workplace is valuable. This is an ideal business tool to show to potential "employers".

ORGANIZED TO BE THE BEST!

BY SUSAN SILVER $13.95   434 PAGES   5.5 x 8.5   #B137

Organized To Be The Best! New Timesaving Ways to Simplify and Improve How You Work is the brand-new, fully-revised 2nd edition of this "bible of organization". Organized To Be The Best! helps you put your time, work & life in order. This book gives you hundreds of practical ideas you can use immediately to have a personal organization system for your paperwork, computer, calendar and organizer that's right for your unique needs.

THE PARTNERSHIP BOOK

BY D. CLIFFORD & R. WARNER $24.95   240 PAGES   8.5 x 11   #B105

Many people dream of going into business with a friend. That dream can become a nightmare without a solid partnership contract. This book shows you step-by-step how to prepare an agreement that meets your needs. It covers initial contributions to the business, wages, profit-sharing, buy-out, death or retirement of a partner, and disputes.

Ripe For Plucking! A New D.O.'s Survival Guide

BY Stephen Davidson, D.O. and Eric Dolgin, D.O.

$99.00 77-page manual, disk and 2 audio tapes: **#BAC100**

This is also a useful tool for **ANY** health care professional. The authors share their loving lessons learned in the school of "hardest" knocks to save you years of trial and error. They have compiled an arsenal of form letters which are also on a companion disk (IBM and Mac available). This allows you to easily customize them with your company information or adapt them for your specific needs. Some of the forms include new patient procedures, office policies, dunning letters, dealing with attorneys, collections, accident reports, missed appointment letters, client forms, referral letters, fee schedule increase announcements, handling insurance companies, and much more!

Small-Time Operator

BY Bernard Kamoroff, C.P.A. **$13.95** 92 pages 8.5 x 11 **#B110**

This classic business guide is a technical manual written in an understandable, non-technical style. It includes complete, readable information — information needed to start and successfully operate any small business: permits, licenses, insurance, bank accounts, financing, bookkeeping, taxes, employees, partnerships, corporations, and much more. *Small-Time Operator* is recommended by the U.S. Small Business Administration and the National Society of Public Accountants.

The Teaching Marketplace

BY Bart Brodsky and Janet Geis **$ 14.95** 176 pages 6 x 9 **#B112**

Almost everyone gets the urge to teach. *The Teaching Marketplace* shows how anyone, with or without formal credentials, can break into the teaching profession. *The Teaching Marketplace* details how to design classes, find jobs through schools and businesses, how to market classes independently, and how to build a lucrative sideline career teaching.

The Twig Unbent: Exercises for a Supple Spine

BY Stephen Davidson **$12.95** 30 pages 6 x 9 Spiral **#B120**

The Twig Unbent offers 20 safe, easy-to-follow, gentle movements and positions to help strengthen and loosen your spine. These are the same spine and body stretching exercises that respected Osteopathic Physician, Robert Fulford, D.O., developed during 40 years of clinical trial and error to help patients throughout the world!

This book is a great adjunctive product for your practice. You can sell it to your clients or just photocopy the appropriate exercises, use the handy space for personal recommendations, and send them home with your clients. These exercises are so clearly illustrated and described that you'll save hours in repeated demonstration, question and answer time.

The Ultimate Hand Book: Self-care for Bodyworkers and Massage Therapists

BY Maja Evans **$15.00** 172 pages 6 x 9 **#B140**

The Ultimate Hand Book addresses the various levels of burn-out — physical, psychological, spiritual, and financial — and discusses ways to deal with the underlying causes. It is designed to assist hands-on healers in maintaining a high level of professionalism and enthusiasm in a demanding career.

The Zen of Hype

BY Raleigh Pinsky **$99.00** 8-Tape Audio Package **#A171**

Raved about by AudioWorld and many magazines, this tape series makes public relations understandable, fun and applicable for small to large businesses alike. It teaches creative tactics to make yourself visible in a way that forwards your goals and your business.